This book is to be returned on
or before the date stamped below

CANCELLED

CANCELLED

30. MAY 1995

CANCELLED
28 MAR 1996
CANCELLED
-6 APR 1998

UNIVERSITY OF PLYMOUTH

ACADEMIC SERVICES
PLYMOUTH LIBRARY
Tel: (0752) 232323
This book is subject to recall if required by another reader
Books may be renewed by phone
CHARGES WILL BE MADE FOR OVERDUE BOOKS

11. FEB 1994

THE EUROPEAN PARLIAMENT

To Barbara

The European Parliament

JOHN FITZMAURICE
BSc., MSc

SAXON HOUSE

© John Fitzmaurice 1978

 British Library Cataloguing in Publication Data

Fitzmaurice, John
  The European parliament.
  1. European Parliament
  I. Title
  328'.3'094   JN36

  ISBN 0-566-00168-3

Published by
Saxon House, Teakfield Limited,
Westmead, Farnborough, Hants., England

ISBN   0 566 00168 3

Printed in England by
Itchen Printers Limited, Southampton

Abbreviations

Lab.	Labour
Con.	Conservative
SPD	Socialdemokratische Partei Deutschlands
PSC/CVP	Parti social chrétien (Belgian Christian Democrat Party)
UDR	Union des Démocrates pour la République. Since October 1976, RPR - Rassemblement pour la République.
RI	Republicains Indépendents
UDE	Union des Democrates européens (UDR Group in the European Parliament 1965-73)
DEP	Democrates européens pour le Progrès
EP	European Parliament
EEC	European Economic Community/European Community
MEP	Member of the European Parliament
mua	Million units of account
SF	Socialistisk Folkeparti (Socialist People's Party)
MRC	Movement des Radicaux De Gauche

Introduction

Direct elections may be a crucial crossroads in the short life of the European Community. They offer a choice and, almost for the first time, an open and democratic choice to be reached, it is to be hoped, after a full public debate.

Direct elections are though elections to the European Parliament. This central fact should not be lost sight of in considering the novel phenomenon of European elections. The Parliament is itself central to the debate. One can after all hardly be against elections; one can only be against direct elections to the European Parliament, because of what the European Parliament is, is not, or might become, could or could not do to the Community as a whole. Indeed, as we shall see, these are the very issues which recur in debate in every member state.

The present part time, 198 member nominated Parliament is one of the four institutions of the Community together with the Commission, the Council of Ministers and the Court of Justice. The first three are the executive or policy making institutions. The decision making process, which many observers in the 1960s described as a dialogue à deux has now become much more a triangular dialogue, with Parliament acting less as a permanent ally of the Commission and more and more as an even handed and independent actor. As yet the weight of the Parliament is by no means equal to that of the other two institutions, but direct elections will reinforce a tendency which is already evident.

The decision making process is not monolithic or autocratic; in fact it is often cumbersome and slow, highly open and complicated, with numerous cross cutting interdependencies which offer maximum leverage for influence and blockage at every level.

1

The present nominated Parliament has a modest, but growing role in Community affairs. It came into being without a specific role. It was a symbol of belief in the parliamentary system of government and a symbol of the democratic credentials of the Community. From its earliest days, the Parliament sought to transcend this purely symbolic role by making a reality of the few powers that it had been given and to acquire new powers when the political climate permitted it.

In the classical sense it is not a Parliament at all, but for all that, its importance should not be underrated. It has as we shall see real power in the budgetary field and can criticise, encourage and influence Council and Commission by involving itself in the continuous dialogue by which Community decisions are reached.

The decision making process is an organised and structured dialogue. It is a continuous dialogue because in reality decisions are reached by consensus; it is structured because there are clear and legally binding procedural aims; it is organised because the Commission exists to promote decision making in the European interest. The Commission normally launches the dialogue with a proposal to the Council based both on a legal provision in the Treaty and on some objective economic and social need.. The form of the proposal will already take into account many political, economic and technical realities. The Commission then has a key role in consensus building in the Council of Ministers which has the final power of decision. The discretion of Commission and Council is not free and unfettered. There are constraints: Community law, powerful interests, the international environment, internal political constraints and the European Parliament.

Parliament is a constraint particularly for the Commission. Parliament can censure the Commission which creates a relationship of political responsibility. Thus, ultimately, Parliament can control the Commission. As a result, in many cases, the Commission must modify its proposals to meet parliamentary objections. Of course the Council is not obligated to take these amendments into account, but increasingly mechanisms for dialogue between the two institutions are being developed, especially where expenditure would be involved, which will have the effect of greatly increasing parliamentary influence with the Council.

The European Parliament has shown itself to be a flexible and adaptable institution. It has shown itself to be capable of remarkable growth and development. Seen in a historical perspective its achievements over the last two decades are considerable. It has built up a parliamentary tradition, party groups have come into being; it has inserted itself into the institutional and political dialogue with the Commission and the Council of Ministers and increased, albeit modestly, its formal powers in the budgetary field. All this has been achieved in a climate often hostile to its endeavours. However, its development has often been uneven, almost haphazard and random, without any overall vision.

Direct elections will have an impact beyond the realm of the European institutions. As we shall see, the debate has in some countries become inextricably bound up with domestic politics. The decision to hold direct elections has, again as we shall see, brought the political parties and organisations (e.g. trade unions) to react to this new political forum. They must decide what relevance to their political objectives it has; they must decide how to intervene in the debate.

If the opportunity offered by direct elections is to be seized, the political forces of the member states must play their free part in the process and must adapt themselves to this new trans-national dimension of politics. New programmes and new organisations, new forms of trans-national cooperation between parties will have to be created.

The future of the European Parliament is crucial to the future of the communities as a whole. The European Parliament is the political institution of the Community _par excellence_ and remains the last hope for the Community obtaining a real political dimension. It has not always been so. At earlier stages in the Community's development other means of attaining a political dimension could have been - and indeed were - envisaged. As examples one can cite the attempts to create a political community in 1952, the abortive European Defence Community and on a different plane, the Fouchet plan and its successive refinements. More recently the 1972 Paris Summit concept of a European Union and the related Report of Belgian Prime Minister Tindemans have been the latest in a long line of attempts to create a political community from the top. Over time the immediate objectives, the building bricks and the cement of such a proposed community may have varied considerably, but the basic concept has been remarkably constant. The political community would have been created by a new inter-governmental agreement, a qualitative step going beyond the organic development of the integration process. The political community or union would have been created as _deus ex machina_, existing alongside, or else subsuming the existing European institutions. It is clear that this approach will not work and the negative and almost embarrassed reaction to the Tindemans Report serves to illustrate this fact only too well.

The Parliament offers a different possibility; the possibility that a political dimension and eventually a political community will arise out of the existing institutions which will gradually become politicised. It should be emphasised that this approach is radically different from the neofunctionalist belief that economic integration will automatically lead to political integration. What is suggested here is that successive acts of will on the part of the Community electorate would gradually and pragmatically build up a political community. Direct elections are then in this line of reasoning a necessary, but by no means sufficient element in the process of development which

4

could lead to a qualitative change in the relations between Community institutions and between the Community and the member states. In this model there is no brusque change. Governments and peoples are not confronted with the stark choice of either accepting massive immediate transfers of authority to supra-national institutions or abandonment of the Community experiment. Much indicates that public opinion desires a 'middle way'. No one can say at this stage whether such a middle way is possible or whether the progressive development of the European Parliament, especially once directly elected can serve as a vehicle for bringing it about. This remains to be seen. Examination of this hypothesis will be a major concern of this book.

The prospect of direct elections has also had an impact outside the Community, not least in the candidates for membership, Greece, Portugal and Spain.

Nowhere is this reaction more evident than in the prospective members. More than for the three new members of 1973, their motives are political. All of them have recently emerged from long periods of dictatorship. Their restored democracies are fragile plants. Membership in a democratic Community is seen as an important support for their own democracies. These countries desire integration into the political, cultural and foreign policy spheres of the Community. Not surprisingly, they place great emphasis on full participation in the institutions, which they wish to see develop. Mr Caramanlis, the Greek Prime Minister, for example endorsed the Report of Mr Tindemans on European Union wholeheartedly, which was more than most of Mr Tindemans' colleagues did. The Spanish democratic forces and particularly those of the Left and Centre Left see Spanish entry to the Community largely as a political necessity for which they are even prepared to make economic sacrifices. For example, at a recent colloquium 'La Espana democratica y Europa' held in Madrid in June 1976, Mr Tamames of the Spanish Communist Part (PCE) proposed that the peoples of the candidate states should be given some

representation, if only a consultative status in the
directly elected Parliament, as from 1978 irrespective
of the fact that they would not yet be members of the
Community.

He considered that the elections '....would
consecrate the democratic rupture at the European
level'. It is clear that he saw the Parliament and
the forthcoming elections in a political perspective -
that of the cooperation of progressive forces in the
whole of Western Europe.

Governments and political parties outside the
Community have not reacted in detail, nor could this be
expected. Their attitude has been conditioned by their
attitude to the Community in general. Undeniably, the
decision to hold direct elections was taken in the
outside world as a sign that the Community still
retained political ambitions in keeping with its
original aims. The issue of direct elections has in
some sense become a symbol of the political health of
the Community; any failure to implement the decision
within a reasonable time, low turnout in the elections,
or disinterest by the parties would on the contrary
have a negative impact in the world outside. There is
less interest in the details or in the limitations with
which the Parliament will still be surrounded, than in
the important political symbolism represented by a
European election.

These kinds of views are interesting because they
point up quite clearly the political significance of
direct elections. Outside observers regard the move
towards direct elections as a significant political
development and evidence of continued political will on
the part of the member states. For them it is a
positive sign among many negative signs. For the
candidate countries, this goes further. For them, the
decision to hold direct elections is some evidence that
the Community is, or may become the political Community
that they hope to join.

Pragmatism of course has its limits. Every so often

pragmatic development requires a fresh impulse. The Treaties are unclear as to how far and how fast Parliament should develop and indeed in what direction. The time is coming when a fresh impulse is urgently needed. Little or no immediate advance in the powers and responsibilities of the Parliament can be expected without a prior increase in its political weight such as could result from election by universal suffrage. In the long run, even those who would oppose more supra-national developments and would see the Parliament more as an organ of democratic control would have to admit that without an increase in legitimacy, its ability to perform even that relatively modest function would be compromised.

Parliament faces a political impasse. Direct elections do however offer a way forward. There is no certainty in this because so much will depend on the outcome of the political debate which will now take place. Already though, the debate about whether direct elections should take place has posed the issues fairly clearly. The debate is about the future powers and role of the Parliament. The question is, can direct elections give the Parliament a new impetus, a new authority and a new influence? Can an elected Parliament play its part in developing the Community? These are the issues to which we shall address ourselves.

Direct elections will not create new institutions. The European Parliament already exists. It has existed for over twenty years. The directly elected Parliament will have no more formal powers than the nominated Parliament which it replaces. It will have to build on the foundations which have already been laid; it will have to create pressure for more powers through its actions, using the existing powers as levers to move to the next stage of development of the institution. It is therefore vital to understand what exists: that is, not only the limitations of the present powers of the Parliament, but also their potentialities for future development.

1 The European Parliament in the decision making process

The European Parliament is one of the four institutions of the European Community and as one of the three policy-making institutions is fully integrated into the Community process. It is involved in the annual budgetary procedure from September to December each year. It gives its opinion in the form of a detailed resolution, often containing specific (and sometimes technical) amendments, on all major items of Community legislation. It is informed of important negotiations with other countries and gives its views on proposed agreements. It conducts its own 'parliamentary diplomacy' through interparliamentary delegations. It is involved in the day to day control of the work of the European Commission through its committees, through written and oral questions and debates in the plenary sessions. As a last resort it may dismiss the Commission by voting a motion of censure.

Its task is primarily that of providing a democratic input into the Community decision making process and providing an on-going forum for debate on Community matters in which the whole range of political opinion in the Community - including British anti-marketeers - can be heard. It serves as a respectable and democratic forum outside the immediate control of the governments and accountable to the wider public. It is thus able to perform an important and precious function.

In much of its work it can only be persuasive, since it will have few formal powers to impose its view. The importance of often reiterated common sense backed by democratic weight and appropriate use of the publicity weapon should not be underrated (nor of course overrated). Where the Parliament does succeed

it is most often by playing an ever more active part
in the numerous 'dialogues' which dominate Community
procedures: dialogues with the Commission at the
early drafting stages; dialogues with the Council; the
triangular dialogues with the Commission and Council.

The role of the European Parliament in these
dialogues could not be so extensive if it had no
bargaining power or leverage such as derives from the
formal powers that it does have and from the publicity
weapon. This is particularly true in matters where
expenditure is involved. The strategy is to be
prepared to use its powers in defence of a point of
view, being prepared if need be to make itself an
obstacle to the smooth flow of procedures. Parliament
must therefore have a point of view and make it known
persistently and logically, at the same time using its
powers - or the threat of their use - to obtain a
hearing and exert leverage in dialogue with the other
institutions.

Any sound appreciation of the present powers of the
European Parliament must then proceed from an
understanding of both the extent and the limitations
of its present powers. These can be broadly divided
into three categories.

POWERS OF CONTROL

The Parliament has according to the laconic
formulation of article 137 of the EEC Treaty,
'supervisory and advisory powers'! In the early days
this was more or less literally accepted in an
accounting sense of ex-post facto control. The ECSC
Treaty limited the right to pass a motion of censure
against the high authority to the presentation of the
general report. Gradually these control powers have
become more extensive both in the ex-post and prior
sense. The main instruments of control are:

Committee discussion. Here Commission officials can
be closely questioned in private closed sessions.

Questions. As we have seen MPs make considerable use of their right to ask questions. About 900 written questions were asked last year (the largest number coming from the socialist group), 80 oral questions with or without debate and some 220 questions in question time.

Debates on reports. Such as the Annual Report, the Report on the Social Situation, on the Economic Situation, on the EAGGF (both sections), on the Social Trend, on the Regional Trend, on Competition, to name only the most important.

Financial control. This aspect has in the past had much less attention than it deserved. Members who did not have the traditions of the Public Accounts Committee to draw on seemed to feel that this was both rather excessively technical and lacked political 'sex appeal'. However, unrelenting British pressure from a whole series of MPs: Mr Pounder, Mr Shaw and Sir Peter Kirk on the Tory side and Lord Bruce and Tam Dalyell on the Labour side have kept this issue in the forefront. Now a Treaty amendment has been made, and an Audit Court has been set up to replace the present much weaker Control Commission. This Audit Court will report to Parliament which is to become solely responsible for giving the Commission a discharge on its execution of the budget and closing the accounts for a financial year. A subcommittee of the budgets committee has been set up (Mr Shaw and Mr Dalyell are members) under the chairmanship of Mr Aigner (German – CD), which has already begun to show that such issues are highly charged and can lead to major confrontations with the Commission.

The censure motion. The Treaty provides that Parliament can by a 2/3 majority of those voting and an absolute majority of its members censure the Commission. Only two such motions have been tabled up to now. The reason for the small use of this important power is clear: its practical value is much smaller than it would seem. Of course, it makes the Commission politically responsible to Parliament in an abstract sense, but this responsibility lacks a real effective sanction. Dismissal by a censure motion might not further the aims of Parliament - quite apart from the large majority imposed by the Treaty. The Parliament has no control over the appointment of a new commission and indeed politically Parliament and Commission have been allies against the Council in trying to push integration forward. Only if such an alliance were to break down and if the Parliament could expect to influence the Council on the appointment of a successor commission could the censure motion be an effective weapon.

QUASI-LEGISLATIVE POWERS

On most Community legislation (and draft Council Resolutions, Programmes, etc.) the Parliament is called upon to give an Opinion. One or more of the twelve specialist committees examines the Commission's text and prepares an Opinion for adoption by the plenary. This Opinion may set out general observations and proposed amendments. The Commission must, in the debate, indicate whether it accepts the Parliament's amendments and will therefore modify its proposal to the Council. In principle the Council does not start work on a proposal until the Parliament has given its Opinion. The Opinion is not binding on the Council, but if it is taken over by the Commission it can under article 149 paragraph 2 of the EEC Treaty only be amended by the unanimous vote of the Council. In any case the Parliament can request the application of a 'concertation procedure' with the Council for measures with important financial consequences.

BUDGETARY POWERS

The budgetary procedure is extremely complex and three years' experience has shown difficulties inherent in the intricate checks and balances of article 203 of the EEC Treaty. The essential point is that Community expenditure is divided into two categories which are

11

subject to different procedures and over which the
influence is radically different:

Obligatory expenditure. (Up to 85 per cent of the
Community budget, including the CAP guidance section.)
Defined as 'expenditure necessarily resulting from the
Treaty, or acts adopted in accordance therewith'. Here
Parliament has the right to propose amendments which
the Council must deliberate at the 'second reading'
stage. At present it must find a qualified majority to
accept such amendments. Under a recent Treaty
amendment the Council will have to find a qualified
majority to reject such amendments.

Non-obligatory expenditure. (e.g. Social Fund,
Research budget, Regional Fund after 1978 etc.) The
Council and the Parliament do not agree on the
classification of expenditure, consequently certain
'grey areas' exist. The Court of Justice has never
ruled on this question. On this non-obligatory
expenditure, the Parliament has the last word, subject
to certain fairly strict limitations. It can reaffirm
by a three-fifths majority amendments rejected by the
Council at its second reading. The total increase
permitted for non-obligatory expenditure is fixed by
the Commission each year on the basis of certain
statistical indicators (normally about 15-20 per cent
of the mass of last year's non-obligatory expenditure).
The Parliament's margin is, in accordance with
complicated rules at least half this percentage.
Within this limit, it freely disposes of
appropriations.

Rejection of the budget. At the end of the procedure,
the Parliament may, for serious reasons, reject the
budget as a whole. In which case the procedure must
be recommenced. As a result, the budget would not be
adopted at the start of the financial year. The
Treaty then allows one-twelfth of the previous year's
appropriation to be spent per month, per chapter of
the budget. In a period of high inflation, this could
involve a real reduction in expenditure, which could
cause serious problems. Thus total rejection could be

a financial, as well as a political, sanction.

COMPOSITION

The present European Parliament has 198 members chosen
from the nine national parliaments. Each of the four
larger member states (France, Germany, Italy and the
UK) send 36 members, Belgium and the Netherlands 14
each, Denmark and Ireland 10 each and Luxembourg 6.
Norway, if it joined the Community, was to send 10
members. The first Common Assembly of the Coal and
Steel Community had 78 members and the EP of the six
had 142 members (with Luxembourg representation always
static at 6).

Representation is not based on any clear and
uncontroversial criteria which could have served as a
basis for apportioning seats in the directly elected
Parliament. There has always been a strong over-
representation of smaller states and population has
only played a relatively minor role in apportionment of
seats. In the Coal and Steel Community the major
member states received 4 seats each and Luxembourg 6
seats in recognition not of its size, but of its
important steel production capacity. In the European
Parliament a variety of criteria have seemingly been
applied: size and population, which gives an equal
number of 36 seats to the four (originally three)
larger member states; maintenance of prior rights (the
case of Luxembourg), adequate naming of committees and
broad representation of political forces. Only in the
debate in Britain on apportionment of seats in the
directly elected Parliament has the argument about
regional representation arisen with any degree of
force, even though several countries have more or less
directly sought to ensure representation in the
delegations for well defined regions (Flanders,
Wallonia, Bavaria, Berlin, Sicily, Sardinia, the South
Tyrol German population).

One can consider the composition of the Parliament
(and its national delegations) from a variety of

points of view:

> Regional representation
> Professional representation
> Party representation at European and national
> level.

The table below shows the number of identifiable regional representations in each of the national delegations. Not very surprisingly, apart from Germany which has a regional party (the CSU), the largest number came from countries such as Belgium, the United Kingdom and Italy which have shown the greatest concern for regional problems in recent years.

	Total Delegation	Number of Regional representations
Belgium	14	14
Denmark	10	–
France	36	3
Germany	36	8
Ireland	10	2
Italy	36	8
Luxembourg	6	–
Netherlands	14	–
United Kingdom	36	9

The British parties have been careful to ensure that their nominees represented the main constituent parts of the United Kingdom, and a very clear balance has been sought in the British delegation as a whole.

The professional balance in the Parliament is not that different from that found in continental national parliaments: large numbers of civil servants, lawyers and academics. However, what does emerge from an examination of the professions of members is the large number of members having connections with agriculture, transport, coal and steel – the main areas where the Community has developed some common policies and where the European Parliament consequently has some potential influence, if not actual power. The current membership of the Parliament includes the following professional breakdown:

    agriculture
    industrialists
    lawyers
    trade union officials
    academics

The political breakdown of the Parliament depends at present on the policy of national parliaments in nominating their delegations. At the moment, the Parliament is relatively representative. Apart from the Belgian Volksunie (Flemish language party) no sizeable national political party is denied representation in the European Parliament. This has not always been so. During the 1950's and the 1960's the French and Italian parliaments selected members only from the majority parties or else allocated a token representation to some opposition parties (the French socialists were long under-represented during the Vth Republic) and above all excluded their powerful Communist parties. Since 1969 and 1973 respectively, the Italian and French communist parties have achieved representation in the European Parliament. At the present time there are members of 49 different national parties in the European Parliament. These members sit in six political groups of which five represent the main political 'families' which are found in the Community:(1)

Socialists	(12 parties from 9 member states)
Christian Democrats	(12 parties from 7 member states)
Liberals + allies	(12 parties from 8 member states)
Conservatives	(2 parties from 2 member states)
Communists + allies	(5 parties from 4 member states)

The sixth group, the European Progressive Democrats group, has members from three national parties and three member states. It does not represent a political

family in the normal sense since it contains
Gaullists, Irish Fianna Fail and the Danish Progress
Party of Mr. Glistrüp (with its almost poujadist anti-
taxation and anti-bureaucracy platform).

Other members come from three regional parties,
including the single SNP member and from the Italian
Moviemento Sociale Italiano (far right). These
members do not belong to any political group.

The socialist group has now become the largest
political group but is far from having an absolute
majority. Indeed, except in the high tide years of
Christian Democracy in the 1950's (when it should be
remembered that nomination procedures favoured centre-
right pro-European and hence Christian parties) no
party has come close to that goal.

PROCEDURE

Much excellent literature exists on the procedure of
the Parliament and it is only intended here to briefly
recall how the Parliament works and the most recent
procedure innovations which may give us some guide to
possible future developments.

The Parliament is in essence a continental
parliament as is to be expected in a body whose
traditions derived from the common parliamentary
heritage of the original six and most particularly
from the French IVth Republic. These traditions were
rapidly built up first in the common assembly of the
Coal and Steel Community (1953-58) and then in the
European Parliament and were well entrenched by the
time of enlargement. Up to now only some limited
grafting of Westminster-style has been achieved, and
that not always harmoniously.

A number of essential differences from British
practice must be pointed out in order to facilitate
understanding of how the Parliament works. The full
plenary Assembly has tended to play a somewhat formal,

even ritualised role in proceedings, debate here having been effectively emasculated by compromise and consensus arrived at in committee. The role of committees is vital in parliamentary procedure. The rules provide that as a general principle no matter can come to the floor unless reported out by a committee. Debates are not on a proposal from the Commission itself, not even on resolutions tabled by MPs, but rather on the committee's report on them. Exceptions exist as they do to every rule, and these have under British pressure become even more numerous, but the principle remains.

The best way to understand the role of committees and other organs in the European Parliament is to follow progress of an opinion through the parliamentary maze. The typical activity is giving an opinion on a proposal for Community legislation. Some nineteen different articles of the Treaty provide for obligatory consultation of the European Parliament; in recent years council on Commission has consulted Parliament over a wide range of other texts: Commission proposals, draft council resolutions, memoranda, 'communications' to the council containing few or even no formal proposals. Parliament now considers nearly every Community text of any importance. The only real outstanding grievances in this area are the procedure for consultation on agreements with third countries (the so called 'Luns/ Westerterp procedure'), frequent late consultations and the frequent absence of adequate data on the financial implications of a proposal.

When received, the President must allocate a proposal to a committee(2) as the main committee in charge of the proposal. Where the subject matter so requires, other committees may be asked to give the main committee an opinion. These frequent references to the budgets committee and legal committee for specialised opinions on the financial and legal aspects of proposals. Indeed, outside the budget itself and staff questions, the Budgets Committee has almost entirely a 'derived' competence.

Since a very recent rule change, committees now have
two possible avenues open to them.(3) For minor,
routine proposals - and these are frequent in the
tariff and agricultural fields - the procedure without
report can be adopted. If lists of proposals suitable
for such treatment, drawn up by the chairman and
secretariat are not objected to, these can go forward
to the plenary without report or debate; if no single
member objects on the floor of the house, such matters
are deemed to have been given a favourable opinion 'on
the nod'. One objection returns the matter to
committee for substantive treatment.

On more important issues, a rapporteur is appointed
to draft a report and steer debate both in committee
and in plenary session. Rapporteurs are important
figures. Since members cannot study all matters they
must rely on rapporteurs to do so. A rapporteur must
report what was the majority (or consensus) view of his
committee, but he has considerable room for manoeuvre.
Indeed his first draft sets the parameters of debate.
Furthermore, both in committee and plenary, he has
certain procedural advantages: he can demand the
floor, as often as he wishes and he always is first, to
express an opinion on amendments after they have been
moved. Furthermore, certain long serving MPs have
virtually become standing rapporteurs on certain issues
on which they will always be appointed to report, for
example, the late Mr Vals on wine, Mr Brouwer and now
Mr de Koning on farm prices, Mr Spénale on budgetary
powers, Mr Schwörer on insurance questions. Of course,
important rapporteurships are coveted and are the
subject of fierce negotiations between the political
groups. Over time the number and quality of
rapporteurships must be evenly spread over groups and
nationalities. Some recurring rapporteurships such as
the budget rotate between groups and nationalities
(1974 Mr Aigner, German Christian Democrat, 1975 Mr
Cointat, French European Progressive Democrat and 1976
Lord Bruce, British Socialist). The budget rapporteur
also handles all supplementary budgets in 'his'
financial year. It should be noted that, with almost
no exceptions, rapporteurs are only chosen from

members of political groups; independants are not appointed, although no rule forbids this.

The rapporteur may give more or less attention to the preparation of his first draft depending on the importance of the matter. In any case, he is supported by a member of the four or five strong committee secretariat. In extreme cases the work on the report may be almost entirely delegated to the committee secretariat. In other more important matters, the committee may hold a preliminary discussion without a written draft. Here the competent commissioner or senior official of the competent Commission Directorate General may well attend in order to explain the reasons behind the proposal, its scope and form and attempt to disarm any objections before these can find their way into the report. Such an initial discussion may give the rapporteur some initial idea of committee sentiment, but the absenteeism resulting from the dual mandate (membership of both national and European Parliament) and the probable absence of any clear group opinions at this stage - at least on details - may mean that disagreement can still emerge at a later stage in proceedings.

Rapporteurs, assisted by the committee secretariat may enter into close contact with commission services and European and national organisations active in the area concerned (e.g. the UNICE, COPA). After one or two meetings the consensus of the committee will begin to emerge. At each stage commission officials are present and participate fully in the discussion; technically, they cannot of course 'negotiate' amendments with the committee, but in practice they can often influence a committee and may indicate the likely attitude of the commission towards proposed amendments. A number of MPs are usually prepared to follow the commission unless strong reasons prompt otherwise. As discussions proceed they become more and more technical. It is rare that Parliament will refuse a proposal outright as a matter of principle. It is almost equally rare that dissident minorities which have expressed strong opposition to the commission's basic concept will move amendments proposing a totally negative opinion.

Normally the main committee will have the matter on its agenda three or four times and many other committees once or twice. Absence due to the imperatives of the dual mandate (membership of both national and European parliaments) can make final adoption of a report a long drawn out affair. It has happened too that a committee or some members have sought to delay an opinion of which they disapproved. Lord Gladwyn's Report on Defence questions was for this reason long held up in the political affairs committee.

The final stage is the adoption of a draft resolution. Each report consists of an explanatory statement and a draft resolution. The draft resolution only is voted upon. The resolution may be short - 'approves the proposal by the Commission' or long, running up to 30-40 paragraphs. Often a resolution will have to be balanced and even almost contradictory in order to take into account the views of interests, nationalities, political groups and committees. Since the Parliament is consensus minded and seeks to avoid close votes on sharp resolutions, the result often only represents the lowest common denominator of the committee. For the moment though, there is a detectable movement towards greater conflict and sharper definition of political standpoints; how far this will go cannot with certainty be stated.

This is not the place to examine the ideology or cohesion of the groups,(4) nor the frequency of national as against political standpoints, however, some comment on the input into committee decision making is appropriate. Reference has already been made to the 'consensus mindedness' of the Parliament and to the role of the rapporteur. Even communist members have, since becoming a group in 1973, perfectly adapted themselves to the role of rapporteur, with which they would in any case be familiar

from their own national parliaments. Group
standpoints are rare in committee. Members normally
speak for themselves only. At least socialist members
of committees do caucus with the group secretariat
member responsible immediately before a committee
meeting and on some issues such as economic and
monetary union and the previously mentioned report on
defence, speakers have even been known to express an
overt group view in committee. Much more frequent are
mixtures of interest group or national standpoints.
On insurance questions there are members who will
state the particularist German standpoint in committee;
on the directive on the admission of shares to
quotation on the stock exchange, British members were
there to express the view of the City that there
should be no state interference in self policing
arrangements - the traditional City approach. Not
only that, but different committees become the
repositories of certain interests or standpoints and
develop over time a certain 'case-law'. Much of the
debate in Parliament on issues such as the setting up
of the CAP, the Mediterranean policy and the Yaoundé
Association, competition policy and harmonisation can
be seen best in terms of inter-committee conflict.
The Agriculture Committee has stood for community
preference in agriculture; the Development and
Cooperation Committee for special preference for the
Yaoundé (and now Lomé) convention states and the
External Economic Relations Committee for freer trade.
The Legal Committee has until recently always favoured
total as against so called 'optional' harmonisation.

When a report has been completed it is translated,
together with any opinions and circulated. The
enlarged Bureau (President, Vice Presidents and the
chairmen of the six groups) must decide to place it on
the agenda. The rapporteur and committee chairman may
be asked to state a preference, but they can do little
to influence the Bureau.

Once on the agenda, the report will be studied both
in the Commission and in the political groups. On
major items groups will have a general policy line,

21

but the small print will still have to be studied. Some issues will have been studied in group working parties. In any case, at the group meeting on the day of the debate, if not before, the rapporteur in his own group and committee members in other groups will inform their colleagues of the situation. All reports are compromises, but is the compromise acceptable? Should a spokesman be appointed? Should amendments be tabled? How should the group vote? These are the questions to be decided.

In debate, the rapporteur introduces his report and any rapporteurs for an opinion may speak. Group spokesmen take the floor, the largest group first. Mostly they have limited time, say 15-20 minutes each. Then individual speakers (backbenchers) may speak. At the end of the debate the commissioner concerned or a colleague replies to the debate; he usually makes a general statement on the policy of the Commission and will indicate the attitude of the Commission to any amendments which the report proposes to his proposal.

Then a vote is taken, normally by a show of hands; roll call votes are very rare. The voting figures are not announced, only the result. Amendments will also be voted on after being moved and briefly debated. Rejection of a report is rare, although in recent years it has happened more often. The most important recent cases were votes on the 1975 Competition report by Mr Normanton(5) (UK conservative) and the report on Shipping Policy by Mr Seefeld (German socialist) in 1974. Neither of these were opinions in legal sense and so no harm could come from their rejection in the way that rejection of an opinion could leave doubt as to what was the European Parliament's position on the issue. Now the position has been clarified to the extent that rejection returns the dossier to committee. As an alternative to rejection, where there are numerous amendments, where amendments have introduced contradiction or where the report has provoked fairly general opposition, it may be returned to the committee for further study.

Resolutions are sent to the council and commission and are published in the official journal. The resolution cannot be legally binding, of course, though it has political weight. The commission (since 1973) informs Parliament systematically of follow-up action taken on proposals.(6) Since 1971 the commission sends an amended proposal to the council if it accepts amendments; hence Parliament amendments become part of the basic proposal. This means, under para 149(1) of the Treaty, that they can only be unanimously rejected. Perhaps more importantly they gain weight from a psychological point of view. Parliamentary opinions also form part of the dossier of the council working parties, COREPER and the council itself. Council organs do not normally begin to work on a proposal until they have received the Parliament's opinion. Nothing can oblige the council to accept opinions and normally such opinions can be no more than an element in the deliberations of the council. A negative opinion on a proposal which would later require funds to be voted by Parliament might carry more weight than on a proposal without financial implications or coming within the budgetary remit of the council. This consideration has been reinforced since the 1974 Joint Declaration of the Institutions on a concentration procedure. The commission must state whether its proposals are amenable to this procedure. The criteria are mainly that the legislative act must have 'notable financial implications' and be generally 'important'. On such acts the Parliament may demand the application of the concentration procedure if the council intends to depart from the opinion of the Parliament expressed by a large majority. However, as of now, the Rules of Procedure do not define how Parliament is to play its part in this procedure. Then the three institutions would meet and attempt to reach agreement between Parliament (almost as a tenth council member) and the council. The Parliament would meet the full council and not just its president in office. The council still after a reasonable period has the right to enact the legislation in a form which would be unacceptable to Parliament. However, this procedure is an important step in the acquisition of co-legislative rights with the council and was certainly the most that could have been achieved at the time.

Parliament has other procedures too: question time, oral questions with debate, debates on urgent resolutions (not referred to committee). Here the introduction of question time in 1973 was the most important innovation. First introduced just before enlargement, but under British impulsion, this facility has indeed been most and best used by British members, both in asking questions and in asking supplementaries. At first one hour, question time now takes up 1-1/2 hours as first business on the Tuesday and Wednesday of each part session. Proposals are under discussion to have three question times per part session. Closing date for questions to both council and commission is the previous Wednesday; each member is limited to one question. Those must be short as should the answers. The President in office or a commissioner replies and the questioner and at the discretion of the President two or three other members may put supplementaries. Some twenty to twenty five questions are normally answered; any others are given a written answer or put over. Since the 1974 summit, it has been agreed that the President in office should answer questions on the work of the foreign ministers in the framework of political cooperation.(7) An impromptu debate can be demanded on a commissioner's answer, to be held for up to one hour at the end of question time.(8) These debates are relatively rare (they have been held on Spain and on the Commission's controversial 'margarine tax' proposals).

Parliament has held two debates on censure motions (December 1972 and July 1976) one on failure to present proposals, one on Parliament's budgetary powers and the other on policy in the milk sector. Only this last led to a vote. The motion was heavily defeated, receiving only the votes of the conservative group which tabled it and the single SNP member.(9)

At one time there was a spate of urgent resolutions,

mostly on wide ranging political issues such as human rights in Spain, the Middle East or French nuclear tests in the Pacific, over which the Parliament has no direct influence. There now seem to be fewer of such debates.

Another form of parliamentary activity is the tabling of written questions - now fast approaching 1,000 per year - to commission and council. The commission has one month and the council two months to answer.

The Parliament has set in motion a process of continuous procedural review on accession since Peter Kirk presented a memorandum which proposed a number of procedural innovations such as urgent debates on the pattern of SO no.9(10) debates at Westminster, more committee hearings etc. A working party was set up under Mr Schujt and produced some interesting ideas some of which moved slowly through the machine: a form of simplified consultation procedure and some changes in quorum rules. In late 1975 a new committee on rules and petitions was established under the chairmanship of Mr William Hamilton (UK, socialist) with the mandate to review the rules, in accordance with the general orientations which emerged from a 'conclave' meeting of the enlarged Bureau. The committee under the guidance of its three rapporteurs on procedure, Mr Hamilton, Mr Martens (Belgium, Christian democrat) and Mr Yeats (Ireland, European progressive democrats) are engaged in far reaching debate on the rules. Up to now the most important concrete results have been the introduction of the procedure for an opinion without report and a reduction of parliamentary committees' quorum to twenty-five of their membership and tighter rules on proxy voting in committee (this is forbidden in plenary votes). For the future likely innovations are provision for more hearings, proposals for public committee meetings and verbatim reports from committee proceedings, disclosure of voting figures in plenary and in committee and possibly some provision for holding at least one occasional symbolic session in

Brussels. This last proposal is extremely controversial and could only be dealt with in a wider context.

NOTES

(1) Fitzmaurice, The Party Groups in the European Parliament, D.C. Heath 1975.
(2) The Parliament currently has twelve committees:
        Political Committee
        Economic and Monetary Committee
        Budgets Committee
        Legal Affairs Committee
        External Economic Relations Committee
        Agriculture Committee
        Development and Cooperation Committee
        Social Affairs, Education and Youth Committee
        Environment and Public Health Committee
        Regional Policy, Transport and Planning Committee
        Energy and Research Committee
        Rules and Petitions Committee
(3) Rule Z 7 A
(4) Fitzmaurice op. cit.
(5) European Parliament Debates J.O. Annexe No.194,25 September 1975
(6) See Document Com. (73) 999: Practical improvements in relations between Commission and Parliament.
(7) Final Communiqué Point 10.
(8) Rule 4 7 A
(9) European Parliament Debates, OJ no.205, 16 June 1976, p.106.
(10) Standing Order no.9 debates are emergency debates on topics of immediate interest and general importance on the initiative of a backbench MP, at the discretion of the Speaker.

2 National parliaments and the Community

If liberty is indivisible, then so must be democracy. In this sense the activity of national parliaments in relation to the Community must, together with the work of the European Parliament, form part of the overall parliamentary control to which the Community is subject. For this reason, an examination of the contribution made by national parliaments can enhance our understanding of the issues related to democratic control and accountability in the Community.

Furthermore, it is sometimes contended that national parliamentary activity is either in contradiction with a stronger European Parliament, and so undesirable or alternatively that national parliamentary activity ought to fill the void of the 'democratic deficit' which undoubtedly exists in the Community. In this way it is held that national parliaments can be viable long term substitutes for the European Parliament. We shall have to examine these views in the light of the available facts.

National parliaments had not expected to play any role in Community affairs. The German Parliament indeed had a doctrinal aversion to doing so to any strong degree lest the role of the European Parliament be undermined. Gradually, however, the need for national intervention was felt instinctively in national parliaments and ruefully accepted at the European level. This process has been greatly accelerated by the accession to the Community of Britain, Denmark and Ireland, all jealous of parliamentary control.

The prise de conscience came about less through the realisation that a revision of strategy was needed in order to underpin the Community at the national level,

secretariat dealing with liaison with international assemblies, and distributed to all members of parliament.

Such reports are naturally factual and non-partisan in character. Only in the political groups can more incisive information be given, but the extent to which this is actually done varies greatly. In France occasional reports are made to the various political groups in the two houses. In Belgium the PSC/CVP has a party committee (including non-parliamentarians) linked to CEPES (a study centre for European problems) chaired by M Dewulf, an active European Parliamentarian, which follows the work of the European Parliament very closely. The Dutch Labour Party Group in the Second Chamber receives the agenda of the European Parliament sessions in advance, but debate within the group has been cursory or nonexistent and there is no formal reporting back. One of the Arbeitskreise of the German SPD is concerned with external policy, and includes most of the SPD members of the EP. This Arbeitskreis has a small specialised staff, of which one attends all sessions, in order to assist the SPD members in Strassburg and to carry out an information function within the SPD Bundestag Fraktion as a whole. The Fraktion publishes regularly a bulletin for those members who have no contact with the European Parliament, giving a summary of the work of the parliament and especially the SPD members, but also opening its columns to members who wish to present an analysis or opinion on certain problems of a Community character.

When we turn to procedures for control, we find various mechanisms: committees, parliamentary questions, debates. The committee work has been the most effective form of control and breaks down into two main forms: special European Affairs Committees or the use of the normal committees system. In the German Bundestag a special committee, the Integrationsältestenrat, was set up in 1963 and functioned until 1967, being abolished in 1969. It was based on an inter-party agreement and was composed of fifteen members, chosen proportionately to the party strengths in the Bundestag. It was never an organ for controlling ministers in their activity in the Council of Ministers, but was solely concerned with the coordination of initiatives relating to the Community in the Bundestag. Though no doubt a useful and necessary function, its overall impact was small and many considered that the normal informal channels could achieve the same result.

Since 1957 (with a change of name in 1965) the German Bundesrat has had a committee for affairs relating to the European Communities. This committee has a general mandate to draw up and reports on matters referred to the Bundesrat under article 2 of the law of ratification. This committee alone is competent on Community matters, coordinating opinions received from other committees. The position of the Bundesrat is made the more unusual in that it is permitted an observer in council meetings and the Länder maintain a liaison office in Brussels. These special features, together with its small size and character as an 'inter-governmental conference' makes its procedure unique and not exportable to other assemblies.

With the exception of the Danish case, the Belgian Chamber's European Affairs Committee (EAC)(2a) represents the most durable and in some ways the most effective example of such a specialised committee. The EAC was set in 1962 and its terms of reference are found in article 83 of the rules of procedure. It received a mandate to 'obtain all information on the consequences of the application of the treaties in respect to European cooperation, and supervise the execution of the latter and follow the development of the organisations they create'. In particular, the EAC is to examine the reports from the government and the delegations to European Assemblies; require the presence of ministers; present reports on the progress of integration; report to the Chamber on any matter referred to it or otherwise worthy of attention or requiring the intervention of the Chamber by virtue of its constitutional prerogatives. Under article 83(2c) the committee has twenty-three members, who may not be members of the EP. This is to ensure that the EAC extends knowledge of the Communities beyond a small group of experts and 'Europeans'. However, many of the members are past or potential members of the EP (MM Fayat, Glinne, Dewulf have been members of the EAC and EP).

Since 1962 forty to fifty meetings have been held, but these have been rather unevenly spaced: 11 in 1962, 9 in 1963 and only 3 in 1964. It was largely the existence of a state secretary in the Foreign Ministry charged with European Affairs in the period up to 1967 which made for the activism and effectiveness of the EAC in its heyday around 1965-66. This minister developed close relations with the EAC. Other ministers also attended: the Agriculture Minister in 1964 and 1966; Finance, Science and Technology and Foreign Affairs. For example, in April 1967 the Finance Minister spoke on international monetary problems. Joint meetings have also been held with other committees, which have not abdicated their interest in European matters which touch their competence. This committee has for some years been almost totally inactive.

In 1968 the Italian Senate set up a 'Giunta Consultativa' or consultative subcommittee of the Foreign Affairs Committee(3) to which, technically, the Giunta reports. The Giunta has met on average once a month and has discussed matters such as the government report previously mentioned, which led to a full debate on the floor in 1969 for the first time. It also discussed agriculture and the law delegating powers to the government to implement Community legislation. As in Belgium and Germany the Giunta does not control or coordinate the work of other committees, which retain an interest in Community matters.

In Denmark(4) entry to the Community was strongly opposed, not least by the Socialist People's Party and by minorities in the Social Democratic Party and the

Radical Party (some 31 MPs). The 'social contract'
under which entry was approved at the referendum was a
limited one: integration was to be restricted to the
present treaties. These special factors, together with
a tradition of parliamentary involvement in foreign
affairs led inevitably to the installation of powerful
control machinery. The instrument of the Folketing
(single chamber parliament) is the Market Relations
Committee (MRC). This seventeen member committee
receives, fortnightly, a list of Commission proposals
from the government of which the important ones are
sifted out for consideration with the minister
concerned. The minister presents to the MRC the
mandate that he proposes to take with him to the
Council of Ministers, and if so required presents a
written statement. The MRC may take the advice of
other specialised committees, and in particular the
Udenrigsnaevnet (foreign affairs committee). If at the
end of the discussion there is no majority in the MRC
against the proposed mandate, then the minister may
negotiate on that basis. If the Commission's proposal
is changed in the course of the discussion in the
council, then the minister must reconsult the
committee, even if only by telephone from Brussels.
The MRC does not report back to the floor of the
Folketing - its members are usually their party's
spokesmen on EEC affairs and so have the confidence of
their party groups, to which they may report. The MRC
thus has a very considerable power of co-decision with
the minister in EEC questions which has not yet
diminished in spite of the time which has now elapsed
since the controversy over EEC membership. This is
without doubt the strictest form of control especially
because it is a form of prior control in detail,
unknown in other member states.

In the United Kingdom(5) the matter of parliamentary
control over EEC legislation looms very large and has
assumed the most systematic and detailed character of
any member state except Denmark, where the political
impact is probably much greater. Already during the
passage of the European Communities Bill, the
opposition sought to write in various safeguards which

were not accepted by the government. In December 1972 both Houses set up select committees to study the problems of scrutiny; both committees reported about a year later having taken evidence in several other Community member states. The recommendations were similar with the Commons placing more weight on the need for floor of the House debates and less weight on detailed scrutiny by a permanent specialist committee. The Lords proposed a committee (and subcommittees) with a strong chairman and small expert staff to give detailed examination to draft Community Acts, to hear ministers, civil servants and outside evidence with a view to make detailed reports to the House for debate. The Commons select committee proposed the more limited role of recommending proposals for debate. A number of other proposals were made on 'European' PQs and on general 'supply' debates on the EEC.(6)

The two committees were set up in May 1974(7), but were hardly active until after the October general election, which swamped them in a backlog of documents which took about six months to clear up. The Commons committee has sixteen members and since 1975 two subcommittees for initial sifting. The Lords committee now has twenty-one titular members and thirty-six coopted members and seven policy subcommittees.

The Lords committee holds more hearings, receives off the record evidence and employs a small number of specialist advisors. The chairman and clerks undertake a preliminary sifting which eliminates two-thirds of documents. Reports, although they merely recommend debate are often detailed and consider both implications - financial, legal and political - and merits. Since late 1975 some joint hearings have been held with the Commons SC subcommittee.

The Commons committee is more restricted in its terms of reference and so merely recommends proposals for debate or not with little comment.

Once recommended for debate, the government has pledged that no decision will be allowed in Council

before the debate has been held.(8) The debates are
often at a late hour, very short and long delayed.
Debates almost always take place on a 'take note'
motion or in 'bundles' on the adjournment, only rarely
has a substantive motion been tabled which allowed the
House to express a view - though this did recently
happen when the House voted to disapprove some
agricultural measures which Mr Peart nonetheless
accepted in Council. In 1974 the Commons committee
recommended 21 documents for debate, the Lords
committee recommended 12 documents for debate. In
1975 the number was doubled. As of July 1976 there are
58 documents pending debate in the Commons and 10 in
the Lords.

The government has obtained amendment of standing
orders(9) to remove debates on less important items
recommended for debate to a standing committee unless
20 MPs object to that procedure.

It is difficult to judge the efficacy of these
procedures in part because they have so far been
enmeshed with partisanship over the issue of EEC
membership. They undoubtedly represent a modest
increase in parliamentary influence but stop well short
of the strict prior control exercised by the Danish
Market Relations Committee.

The Irish Dail and Senate have set up a joint
committee on European Affairs, composed of 26 members,
with a chairman from the opposition.(10) The task of
the committee, which includes all ten Irish members of
the EP, is to report to both Houses on draft
Regulations and Directives, with particular reference
to administrative or legislative changes which would
be required and their effect on Irish interests. The
committee hears ministers and senior civil servants.
It is intended to set up a number of subcommittees.
Some difficulties have arisen in that the committee
members consider that the government has not provided
them with adequate information.

In France the constitutional position makes the

formation of new committees difficult, since article 43 limits each House to six. This has not prevented the establishment, in 1967, of a less formal body, Le Groupe d'Action pour l'Europe. This group is open to all deputies and some 80 have joined. It has no formal powers and no place in the rules of the Assembly, but does act as a forum for the dissemination of information and discussion, albeit limited since ministers do not attend and no record is taken of discussions. The Foreign Affairs Committee alone has a special competence for Community matters, but only along with other foreign policy issues.

Special European Affairs Committees have not been an unqualified success. They have had difficulty in attaining sufficient status and attracting a high enough calibre of membership. If they were to include say, the chairmen of all other committees, they would then hold a pre-eminence vis-à-vis the other committees which may not be desired since Community policy is not a neatly demarcated area, but spills over into every domain of national policy. There is another danger that such committees will become the preserve of EP members and a small group of specialists, cut off from the main stream of parliamentary opinion. This is not to deny their usefulness: they have become centres of coordination, of dissemination of information and for discussion, pursuing an educative function. However, severe limitations must be recognised, except in the Danish committee and the German Bundesrat, where a clear and unequivocal central role has been given to the committee.

The second form of committee scrutiny, found in the German Bundestag, in the Dutch Second Chamber and to a lesser extent in the Italian Chamber, is leaving scrutiny to the normal committee structure, each in its own sphere of competence, without central coordination. The Dutch Second Chamber relies on the activism of certain members and the normal specialised committees to do the job. The Foreign Affairs budgetary committee does not act as, nor even seek to act as, a

European Affairs Committee. It has both wider and narrower functions: it deals only with the general aspect, providing in May/June of each year the forum for a set piece debate on the annual report presented by the government; on the other hand it deals with more general foreign affairs matters. It does not control or coordinate the discussion of Community questions in the Second Chamber. The Dutch specialist committees (those on Agriculture, Commerce and Finance and Transport) have developed a strong interest in the Community aspect of their work. Politically important proposals of the Commission are considered by the responsible committee in the presence of the competent minister, who will inform the committee, in closed session, of the position of the government on the draft, its reservations and the urgency which will be accorded to the proposal. The committee will hold an exchange of views with the minister and may challenge him on some points and may seek certain undertakings. The committee will then expect a report on the deliberations of the Council and, if the matter comes up at several Council meetings an interim report on progress, when the minister may be pressed hard to change his tack or to insist on certain basic principles. This procedure stops well short of the degree of control exercised by the Danish Market Committee. Even this ideal is seldom attained, however the Dutch committees are less likely than others (except the Danish committee) to be content with ex post facto control and more likely to be able to insert themselves into the decision making process at a formative stage, at least on important matters. (11) All this control is carried out in committee; especially since 1967 there has been very little debate on the floor of the House.

The German Bundestag (in spite of an experiment with a special committee) employs a more formalised version of the Dutch system. Under article 2 of the law of ratification, all Commission proposals are sent to the Bundestag (and Bundesrat) by the Federal Government and then referred by the Bundestag to one committee as the leading committee 'federführender Ausschuss' and

such other committees as might be involved are asked
to give an opinion. Ministers are summoned before,
during and after Council deliberations. The report
will either merely take note of the proposal if it is
unimportant and technical or may instruct the
government in detail on the line it should follow and
the amendments it should seek. In special cases
(value added tax proposals and those on beer) the
committee concerned may seek information from a wide
range of outside interests and even travel to Brussels
for discussions with Commission officials. Few
reports have led to full dress debates on the floor
(only those dealing with major agricultural proposals
or economic and monetary union), but others may lead to
a brief exchange of views or the presentation of
observations when the report comes up for formal
adoption by the Bundestag. This procedure achieves
the same results as the Dutch procedure, but has the
same drawback in greater measure – that is the danger
of clogging up the system with detail in a morass of
technical matters and the problem of controlling a
fluid and complex activity like the deliberations of
the Council, bearing in mind that each national
parliament can only call its own minister to account
and not those of other member states.

These forms of control are supplemented by other
forms such as debates and parliamentary questions.
Questions are mainly useful for eliciting information
or drawing attention to a matter. There are perhaps
only about 100 written parliamentary questions per
year on Community affairs in the legislatures of the
larger member states except Britain where the figure is
significantly higher. There has, though, been a
tendency for the number to increase over the last few
years.(12)

The questions, especially in Germany and France are
likely to concern agriculture, but a large number of
the Dutch questions are what might be called
'institutional questions', such as the competence of
Community institutions, the supremacy of Community law,
procedure in the Council, the powers of the European

Parliament, fulfillment of treaty obligations. Dutch
questions are more likely to have been put from a
'European point of view', that is asking the
government to support Community institutions, carry
out obligations under Community law, rather than the
defence of national interests and here the Dutch
members of the European Parliament (and in the past
particularly Vredeling, Oele and Westerterp) have been
particularly important, asking over half the questions
asked in any one year on European topics.

Another means by which national parliaments express
themselves is in the numerous debates on Community
topics. These fall into three broad categories:
formal debates - ratification debates, debates on laws
implementing Community legislation; regular debates -
Foreign Affairs and Agriculture debates and debates on
annual reports; occasional debates - debates on some
unique event or to draw attention to specific problems
(Summit Conference, economic and monetary union,
powers of the EP). Such debates may sometimes be
introduced by a motion or oral question from a
backbench member. Debates are normally set piece
affairs: statements from group spokesmen, from the
minister and finally interventions from backbenchers.
Except in France the debate may be concluded by the
adoption of a motion. In Denmark general debates are
to be organised on a regular basis - two or three times
per year. In Britain too such debates will tend to
increase in number. Several general debates have
already been initiated in the Lords (e.g. on EEC-USA
relations). Otherwise it is clear that such debates
engender little controversy and are relatively
ineffective instruments of control.

However, the role of European Parliamentarians
should not be exaggerated. In Holland, for example,
only Berkhouwer is foreign affairs spokesman for his
party and Vredeling was for many years not labour's
spokesman on agriculture (the post was held by Mr Van
der Ploeg, who was never in the EP). Dutch European
Parliamentarians have not generally spoken in the most
important political debates, such as the debate on the

39

Speech from the Throne opening the parliamentary
session, but have been prominent only in special
debates on European issues. Here one sees the danger
of European questions becoming isolated from politics
in general and the preserve of specialists.

Issues brought up in the European Parliament are
frequently referred to in these debates and the
proceedings of the EP themselves mentioned, but one may
doubt the political punch of such debates: attendance
may be low (as low as 3 or 4 out of 212 in Foreign
Affairs debates in Belgium) and confined to European
cognoscenti. Ministers are not in general required to
give any prior commitment to a line, nor is the House
able to exert control beyond the level of generalities.
The only real exceptions are the pledges given by
Foreign Minister Luns to the Dutch Second Chamber on
the budgetary powers of the European Parliament during
the debate on the 1965 'triptych' proposals and the
similar, but weaker pledge extracted in Germany.

It is difficult to trace in detail issues which have
been 'echoed' in national and European Parliament.
Analysis of every Community act published in the
Official Journal in February 1972 showed no follow up
of a direct character to any such act in the following
four months in national parliaments.

In the Netherlands from 1970-73 some 46 separate
issues were the subject of parliamentary intervention
both in one or other House of the States General and in
the European Parliament, but usually the intervention
was limited to the tabling of a written question.

However, more important than these procedures is the
dynamism and activism of the small number of members of
the European Parliament in the national parliaments.
The European Parliament has only been able to have a
repercussive effect in the national parliaments and
issues have only been echoed from one level to another
where issues have been taken up by members of the
European Parliament, assisted sometimes by a small
group of pro-Europeans who are involved only at the

national level (such as former members of the European Parliament, members of the European Affairs Committees, or former European personalities).

The activism of members varies greatly. It is instructive to take the members of a national delegation and examine what they did in their national parliament that was of European interest. This analysis was undertaken for the French members of the National Assembly for 1971. Of the 24 members, 15 appeared to have made no 'European' contribution and, of the others, 2 had done no more than to ask one written question on a European subject. On the other hand, Monsieur Cousté had been rapporteur for one (minor) matter, had intervened in two major debates, asked two oral questions and six (out of 40) written questions.

On the other hand, certain members have sought to devote themselves almost entirely to the European scene and have thus been particularly active. In Germany one can mention Mr Kriedemann (who may have been denied renomination on the grounds of his European activism). In Italy the PCI members have been largely chosen for their professionalism, moderateness and expertise and have been largely assured of being re-elected and been given the explicit task or working largely in the European arena and bringing European issues up in the Italian Parliament. Danes (particularly anti-marketeers such as Mr Maigaard) are usually of high status in their parties.

However, the main exponents of the European mandate are the Dutch and, in particular, the Dutch Socialists from the Second Chamber such as Mr Labon, Patijn, van der Hek and formerly Mr Vredeling (now Commissioner). The position of the Dutch is exceptionally favourable in that all 150 members of the Second Chamber are elected on a national list system; hence no member has to 'nurse' a constituency or local party organisation. He only has to retain a place near the top of his party's national list. The Dutch Labour Party is prepared to allow some members to devote the major part

of their time to European activity either in the
European Parliament or in the national parliament.

Having examined the procedures which have been
evolved in the national parliaments and the level of
parliamentary activity, we should attempt to reach
some conclusions as to how to evaluate that activity.
It is clear that the attitude of the different national
parliaments has varied greatly. The intensity of
control by national parliaments can be placed on a
continuum:

```
     France   L   B   IRL I   UK   D   NL   DK
                         O
  _____

low                                              high
```

It shows that the intensity and impact of
parliamentary activity is a function more of the
political system than of the procedures: Holland (NL)
and France have almost equally little procedural
devices; the Danish Parliament and the Belgian
Parliament both have European Affairs specialised
committees.

Except for the special case of Denmark, it is only
through the activism of individuals (Vredeling and
Lord O'Hagan come to mind, as do the Wine district
deputies MM Payou, Poudevigne) who have taken up
issues and made them their own. Otherwise the
impression is one of formalism. The character of
'European debates' is that of set piece debates: a
statement by the minister - largely a catalogue of
achievement and occasional statements of position.
Speakers in the debate would deliver polished, academic
exhortatory speeches containing a catalogue of very
general, often unrealistic demands (majority voting,
political cooperation, direct elections). Foreign
Affairs debates are by no means entirely devoted to
Europe: in France Europe may form less than half the
content of Foreign Affairs debates. There is a low
level of politicization, except that opposition
members are inclined to take an overly pessimistic

view of Community developments and hold the government
responsible for that situation. European Parliament
members are by no means as important as might be
thought. Debates with European content may be
classified as follows:

	Party spokesmen from EP	Speakers from EP
General Political debates	No	Few/None
Foreign Affairs debates	No	Few
European debates (Agriculture)	Sometimes	Some/Many
Technical debates (with European content)	Yes	Many

It is clear that the erosion of power of parliaments
at the national level has not (as was hoped) led to
any real compensation through the European Parliament.
As is the tendency at the national level, the
development of the Community has drastically reduced
formal parliamentary control in favour of executive
organs (Council and Commission); the national
parliaments have reacted to this by a certain prise de
conscience, but above all they have reacted in a
patchy and varied manner. It is a long way from
realising that national parliaments are willy-nilly
involved in the Community decision making process and
that there has been an erosion of the powers of
national parliaments and of the quantum of
parliamentary control in general, to taking any
effective action. In most cases this extra step –
towards effective action – has not been possible.

Another source of impetus to action has been that
provided by the various interest groups. On the whole
the membership of the European Parliament, participants
in specialised Community debates (this does not mean
foreign affairs debates, where leading party spokesmen
take the floor) has been limited to 'Europeans' and
agricultural specialists, with a sprinkling of

transport and industrial experts. It is significant
that the greatest sustained intervention in Community
questions from non EP members has come from a small
group of French MPs representing the small wine
producers of the Gard and Herault in the traditionally
left wing South West.

In conclusion it can be said:
1.   The general, global level of parliamentary
        activity is relatively low, both in terms of
        quantity and in terms of political impact,
        but with significant variations from country
        to country and over time. There have been
        troughs and crests of interest: in general
        there was initially little interest, with
        thereafter a build up to a 'high point'
        about 1965, after which (except in the three
        new member states) activity was reduced until
        it was again renewed after 1970. By all
        indicators 'European' activity is well below
        ten per cent of total parliamentary activity.
2.   Activity has settled into predictable annual
        patterns: debates on reports from the
        government or from European Parliament
        delegations, taking place at the same time
        each year; annual foreign affairs (budget)
        debates; agriculture debates. In France (on
        the basis of oral questions with debate) and
        in Germany (on the government's 'Grüner
        Bericht') an annual agricultural debate has
        become a tradition.
3.   Activity is closely linked with interest
        groups who bring pressure to bear on certain
        members to intervene and fuel them with
        information (and indignation). This is
        particularly true of agricultural interests
        (French wine growers) and industries such as
        textiles hit by competition.
4.   Effective intervention by national
        parliaments, with any real hope of
        influencing decisions is - irrespective of
        the actual level of parliamentary activity -
        extremely difficult or even virtually

impossible. The sole, but very real
exception is Denmark. This general point is
borne out both by a study of procedure and
behaviour:

a. there is a problem of the sheer
technicity of much Community legislation and
the strangeness of Community procedures, with
all the resultant problems of timing - when
should national parliaments intervene in the
procedure?

b. the feed-back between the European
Parliament and the national parliaments has
been to a large extent ineffective, both in
terms of the flow of information and in terms
of the real influence of EP members in their
own parliaments and parties. EP members are
to an extent isolated due to the demands made
on their time by the dual mandate system and
due to the fact that other members of the
national parliaments have not shown great
interest in Community affairs, except in so
far as these impinged on certain interests.

c. the difficulty of an accurate
perception of the nature of 'Community
politics'. MPs do not seem able to situate
Community affairs as between foreign and
domestic affairs, thus leaving them in a
limbo, largely the fief of specialists.

d. whatever the procedures used by
national parliaments in their attempt to
control Community decisions (or more
accurately to control their ministers), the
resultant activity is more impressive in
quantity than in impact. Procedural
refinements do not much alter cases. The
vital factor is the nature of the national
political system and the role of parliament
within that system and the ease with which
parliament can adapt itself to the changed
circumstances brought about by Community
membership. From the opposite ends of the
spectrum, Denmark and France both illustrate
this point well.

What measures has the European Parliament itself, as an institution, taken to foster links with the national parliaments? In general one is forced to say that the attitude has been negative. There are, though, reasons for this negative approach; in the first place, unlike the Council of Europe and the Western European Union, which depend entirely on national action to enact their recommendations, the Community has supranational powers of its own which by-pass the national parliaments. This situation has made the need for cooperation less obvious and less intense. By the same token, the 'integrative' nature of the Community decisions is such as to arouse fierce political controversy along the same lines of force in both the European and national Parliament; this means that national parliaments which have a majority of government supporters (in the nature of things) cannot be harnessed to the cause of the European Parliament against their national government, or only rarely. Lastly, there is a doctrinal point; the European Parliament sees itself as a pre-federal and ultimately a federal parliament, replacing the national parliaments in those areas where competences have been transferred to the Community. This implies a slackening of links with the national parliaments rather than closer links. The European Parliament appears to take the view, or at any rate foresee the danger, that increased links with the national parliaments could be institutionally regressive, even as a temporary, stop-gap measure to fill the void arising from the present weakness of the European Parliament.

As a result, the measures which have been taken so far have been, to say the least, tentative, hesitant and ineffective. Two reports(13) have examined this question, but came out against a greater role for the national parliaments. In January 1963 a special meeting was held in Rome at the initiative of Signor Martino, President of the European Parliament. This was a meeting between the presidents of the national parliaments and their secretary generals and those of the European Parliament. This meeting considered how each parliament could better organise its sessions to enable the European Parliament to function better; little was achieved. On the question of giving Community affairs a wider echo in the national parliaments, the final declaration limited itself to vague statements of good intentions - more debates, and so on. The only practical consequence was the designation of 'liaison members' of each national delegation who would meet together to coordinate their work of information and coordination in the national parliaments. This procedure was not effective and soon fell into abeyance. Several subsequent meetings have been hardly more positive. On the initiative of Mr Behrendt, President of the European Parliament, a colloque (Colloque parlementaire européen) was held on 15-16 March 1972, at which there were representatives of the national parliaments and the European Parliament. In the debate statements were made by the national and European party groups on the theme 'The state of European Unification and the role of parliaments'. It is intended that this colloque should become a permanent, annual fixture. Useful points of view were put and some suggestions made, but no firm conclusions were reached.

The Behrendt Presidency also saw the organisation of the symposium on 'European Integration and the future of Parliaments in Europe'. Thereafter interest in such ideas seems to have diminished. Appeals for pressure on national parliaments or coordinated action remain rare and largely rhetorical.

When one turns to actual cases where the Parliament has sought to involve national parliaments, the result is meagre. It has not been done often and it is difficult to be sure whether or not it is in reality a case of a 'private initiative' by an active member of the European Parliament.

The involvement of national parliaments with Community affairs has then been uneven and sporadic. It has either been of an extremely technical character, lost among specialists with little political resonance, or it has been over politicised as a pawn in the debates about Community membership which have raged in the new member states. The 'highs' have corresponded to the periods of the greatest intensity of such debates. Apart from the unique case of the Danish Market Relations Committee the various forms of national parliamentary intervention have found neither an appropriate rhythm of activity, nor appropriate strategic goals.

It is clear that the procedures are often the product of an uneasy compromise between contending forces with different or contradictory aims. For many who support the Community, these procedures are acceptable only as a short term alternative to a stronger European Parliament, as a protection against the charge that there is no democratic debate about Europe. As such then national parliamentary activity is a necessary short term palliative. For anti-marketeers, these procedures are an essential safeguard and a filter. By these means the Community may be kept at arm's length. Such procedures are a desirable alternative to direct elections for many anti-marketeers.

Our survey would suggest that these often ramshackle procedures are doubtful instruments for making up any 'democratic deficit' that may exist in the Community. More often than not they would not meet the expectations of either faction. Above all national parliamentary procedures are almost entirely negative in aim. At all events, they hardly represent a long term alternative to a stronger and directly elected parliament.

NOTES

(1) The EEC: national parliaments in Community decision making, PEP, Chatham House 1971.
(2) For information on Germany see evidence to the House of Lords Select Committee, second report of the Committee on procedures for scrutiny of proposals for European instruments, pp.212-27 and paras 78-82 and second report from the House of Commons SC, pp.97-110.

(2a) J. Gerard-Libois: The Belgian Parliament in the Political System in European integration and the future of parliaments in Europe.

(3) A. Chiti Batelli: 'La Giunta degli affari europei del Senato e i Rapporti fra Parlamento europeo e parlamenti nazionale' in Rivista di diretto europeo, July-September 1969.

(4) For information on the Danish position, see Fitzmaurice, J.: National Parliaments and Community policy making - the case of Denmark, in Parliamentary Affairs, vol.XXIX no.3, Summer 1976, pp.281-92.

(5) There are several useful accounts of the UK situation: H.N. Millar: Parliamentary Influence? The United Kingdom, Parliament and European Communities Policy Making, paper given to the American Political Science Association 1976 annual meeting; Ryan, N. and Isaacson, D.: Parliament and the European Communities in Parliamentary Affairs, vol.18, pp.199-215; Kolinsky, M.: Parliamentary Scrutiny of European Legislation, in Government and Opposition, vol.X, no.1, Winter 1975.

(6) See House of Lords SC Second Report 25 July 1973, and House of Commons SC Second Report 25 October 1973.

(7) See House of Lords Debates, 5 February 1974, cols. 713H.

(8) Mr Hattersley, House of Commons Debates, 11 June 1974, col.1547.

(9) H C D, 3 November 1975, cols.28-113.

(10) M. Robinson, The role of the Irish Parliament, in 'European Integration and the future of parliaments in Europe', pp.82-8.

(11) Niblock, op.cit. 36-8.

(12) For Germany and the Netherlands:

	1962 -3	'63 -4	'64 -5	'65 -6	'66 -7	'69 -70	'72 -3
Bundestag							
Oral questions	13	33	46	20	32	59	
Second Chamber							
Written questions	9	26	11	20	10	67	75

For France:

	1971	1972	1973
Written questions total	48	92	113
of which agriculture	25	72	85
Questions d'actualité total	4	21	11
agriculture	1	15	6
Oral questions & debate total	1	2	3
agriculture	1	1	1
Oral questions without debate	3	4	4
	–	–	–

(13) Strobel Report, Document 110/66-7 and the
Illerhaus Report, Document 118/66-7.

3 Direct elections

Direct elections would be the most important single event in the development of Parliament and perhaps of the Community; more significant even than the cumulative effect of the increases in powers. Direct elections would open a new prospect and offer new opportunities for a new point of departure for a political community. It would be a moment of truth for the Community. Agreement to hold direct elections was indeed a revolutionary event and one fraught with difficulties.

On 20 September 1976 the foreign ministers of the nine signed the act providing for direct elections to the European Parliament and approved a decision which was a solemn declaration of intent to hold those elections in 1978.(1) Although the national ratification procedures and national electoral laws must be completed, and as we shall see this is not an entirely simple matter in some member states, the basic decision has now been taken. This ends a long debate about the matter which goes back to the earliest days of the Community and certainly to 1960. However, it is particularly since the end of 1974 that progress has been discernible, making possible the historic decision of September 1976.

The whole idea of directly elected members of a European Assembly came about almost as an afterthought and by the backdoor. The first Schuman Plan of 9 May 1950 contained no reference to any parliamentary body. In the course of negotiations, several governments made it clear that they could only accept Mr Schuman's proposed supra-national high authority if it was subject to some form of control of which an assembly was to be one element. The idea that members of such a common assembly might be directly elected was to emanate - ironically enough - from the French National

Assembly's foreign affairs committee.(2)

The Treaty of Paris simply provided (article 21) that members would either be nominated or elected by universal suffrage in accordance with procedures fixed by member states. If this procedure had ever been applied by a member state, there could have been a parliament partly elected and partly nominated. In event, this possibility was not used.

On several occasions the Common Assembly drew attention to it and set up a subcommittee under Fernand Dehousse (Belgium, socialist) to study how the Assembly might encourage use of the article. This subcommittee submitted no report and was overtaken by the signing of the Treaty of Rome and the establishment in 1958 of the European Parliament.(3)

The Treaty of Rome contains a much more far reaching provision on direct elections, namely article 138(3) which is worth quoting in full here:

> The Assembly shall draw up proposals for elections by direct universal suffrage in accordance with a uniform procedure in all member states. The Council shall, acting unanimously, lay down the appropriate provisions, which it shall recommend to member states for adoption in accordance with their respective constitutional rules.

This meant that there would be a simultaneous introduction of direct elections in all member states, in accordance with procedures agreed at the Community level, as a further stage in the integration process.

Parliament was not slow to act on the mandate which this proposal gave it. On 22 October 1958 it set up nine and later thirteen member subcommittees again under Mr Dehousse to draw up a draft convention. Mr Dehousse undertook a tour of the national capitals and consulted a wide range of political figures and experts. The group met 20 times for a total of 30 days and presented its report to Parliament in May 1960.(4)

This report is now of no more than historical interest, but it did set the parameters of the discussion and its subsequent treatment showed quite clearly the obstacles which had to be faced - and in some respects still have to be faced.

In a manner, which would no longer be possible now, (5) the allocation of seats was ignored and the number of members representing each country was merely trebled. This decision was quickly the object of severe criticism, particularly in France. Furthermore, a transitional period, linked to the phasing in of the Rome Treaty (ending at the latest in 1970) was provided for. During this period one third of the members were to be nominated and national electoral systems were to apply. In the main, the convention left as much to national rules as possible, but in comparison with the convention actually approved in 1976 was much more dirigiste in approach. This arose perhaps from a greater optimism as to what could be achieved and from a less pragmatic reading of the words 'uniform system' in article 138(3). This provision for a transitional period, too was the object of considerable opposition.

Presented to the Council in May 1960, the convention was never given any serious substantive consideration. General de Gaulle then President of France, was not prepared to accept direct elections which in his view could only lead to an automatic increase in the powers of the Parliament and therefore an erosion of French national sovereignty. Under occasional harassment from the Parliament or pressure from governments of the other five, who favoured detailed examination of the convention, the Council or its subordinate organs would indulge in complicated legal wrangling about the transitional period and the distribution of seats. The French Government also contested the absence of a common electoral system. However, the fundamental objection was one of principle: opposition to the idea of supra-nationality.

The first summit conference of 1961 formed a study group to examine the question of a political union.

The report showed the divergence between 'the Five' and France on the issue of direct elections which became even clearer at the second Bonn summit in July 1961. The European Parliament passed a resolution presented by Mr Pleven on 28 June 1961(6) on political cooperation in which it insisted on the importance of direct elections. In December of the same year, a resolution tabled by Mr Pleven (France, liberal) on the Fouchet Plan demanded elections within three years.

The Council's reply to a written question in April 1963 showed that the disagreement was still just as total.(8)

Parliament returned to the problem in a major debate on Mr Furler's Report(9) (Germany, CD) on the competences and powers of the European Parliament. A resolution was adopted which among other things demanded the rapid approval of the convention. This was, in the aftermath of General de Gaulle's 'veto' on British entry and the collapse of discussions on the Fouchet Plan, increasingly unlikely.

In November 1964 the Italian Government proposed a new summit conference and, as a preliminary, serious consideration and adoption of the convention, with elections taking place before 1970. The Community was soon to enter its most serious crisis - the period of the 'empty chair' during which France withdrew from the Council, largely in order to prevent application of majority voting in the Council. Only the famous 'Luxemburg compromise' got the Community back in business, but the price was its increasing intergovernmentalisation. Clearly no initiative on direct elections could then hope to succeed.

Parliament, more in despair than anything else turned to legal remedies. In May 1968, Mr Deringer (German, DC) and others tabled a motion threatening to invoke article 175 against the Council for failure to take a decision. Almost a year later, in March 1969, Mr Dehousse reported favourable on this initiative and Parliament adopted a resolution to this effect.(10)   It should be noted that during the debate spokesmen for the UDR (Gaullists) opposed this resolution and Mr Habib Deloncle proposed an amendment insisting on the reapportionment of seats on a one man one vote one value basis, obviously a wrecking amendment.

Reacting to this, on 12 May the Council referred the matter to COREPER for study.(11) In fact, since France, the main obstacle, was in the midst of a presidential election campaign, it could do little else. However, from a formalist point of view, this minimum gesture enabled the Council to evade legal action, in that it had 'deliberated' on the convention. In November, the COREPER requested an opinion from the Council's legal service on the issue of the transitional period (now almost over in any case!).

In November 1969 The Hague summit conference communiqué stated laconically: 'the Council will continue to study the question of direct elections.' (12) Parliament in resolution on the summit deplored the absence of a clear timetable and demanded that a dialogue be opened between the two institutions.

The Council agreed to this and itself briefly discussed the matter on 29 September and 14 December 1970. More studies were to be conducted, but the Council's general affairs group always returned to the same contentious issues which it could not solve, of the number and distribution of seats and of a transitional period. It would seem that the efforts to find a solution were sporadic and fitful, for example between December 1969 and November 1970 the general affairs group did not consider the matter at all.

There were three meetings between the President in office and the Political Committee, in July 1970, December 1970 and March 1972. These meetings were unproductive. Other contacts also took place between the two Presidents (Mr Scheel – Mr Scelba in July and December 1970), where the Parliament raised the danger of national projects for elections being adopted and the question of enlargement of the Community. Although

for the Parliament there may have been warning lights
that procedures should be accelerated, they were in
fact likely to cause further delay and confusion. Mr
Behrendt, the new President of Parliament raised the
matter in Bonn and COREPER considered the question on
29 April 1971, but there was no concrete result. By
now, the idea of a joint committee Council - Parliament
was in the air; it was rejected by France at the
Council of 22 July and again in September after
discussions between Mr Pedini (Council President) and
Mr Behrendt in early July. As indicated the meeting of
2 March 1972 produced no results and the summit held in
Paris 1972, including the three new member states, did
not mention direct elections, which was regretted by
the Parliament in its resolution of 14 November 1972.
(13)

There, until after enlargement the matter rested. It
is clear that the 'shuttle' of the years 1969-72
represented little more than a formal going through the
motions. Once it became clear that President Pompidou
was not going to change French policy on this issue and
that the Community was soon to be enlarged, the matter
could in reality not be moved further forward. In any
case, a new approach was opened up, that of more powers
for the Parliament, which was to lead to the Treaty of
Luxemburg of 22 April 1970, increasing to an extent the
budgetary powers of the Parliament, the Vedel report of
1972 and the new proposals of the Commission in June
1973 leading to treaty amendments in July 1974 and
agreement on the concertation procedure. It was fairly
obvious that these changes represented the most that
could be achieved by way of institutional reform at one
time.

As a parenthesis, it should be mentioned that while
all these unproductive moves were being undertaken at a
community level, moves were set in train in several
member states to pass legislation providing for the
election of the national delegation by universal
suffrage, irrespective of the lack of progress on a
community level, which was a return to the sense of
article 21 of the ECSC Treaty. The main drawback of

such schemes was - apart from reprecussions on the campaign for the adoption of the Dehousse convention - that only members of national parliaments could be elected if they were to be eligible to sit in the European Parliament under article 138(1).

Between 1963-70 some 12 different draft bills were tabled; at least one in each member state. Mostly, these bills came from the opposition (Mr Mommer, SPD, in June 1964, Mr Urbany, Luxemburg, communist, in April 1969) and had mainly propaganda objectives. Governments were in the main hostile. In Germany, the SPD bill was rejected by the CDU-FDP coalition and a later CDU bill by the SPD-FDP coalition. Only the FDP were consistent: Belgian and Dutch bills came from members of the governing parties and were given more serious consideration. The opposition of governments, legal difficulties and in Belgium linguistic battles bogged even these efforts down. Two private members' bills have even been tabled in Britain (Lord O'Hagan, cross bench and Clement Freud, liberal, Isle of Ely).

The European Parliament's attitude to these initiatives has been ambivalent; on the one hand they were useful sources of pressure, but on the other hand they could reduce the chance of progress on the Community level. At the lowest point in 1971, the Parliament discarded some of its prudence and sought closer contacts with the authors of such bills and a meeting was organised on 6 October 1971 with the Political Committee.(14)

In May 1971, the Political Committee asked Mr Lautenschlager (German, socialist) to examine whether any revision of the 1960 draft convention was needed. Not only was the transitional period over, substantial criticism had been levelled at the distribution of seats and the Community was soon to be enlarged. The Dehousse formula would, if applied integrally have given a parliament of 594 which would have been too large. On 4 June 1973, Parliament decided to ask the Political Committee to draw up a new report and Mr Patijn (Dutch socialist) was named rapporteur.(15)

At an early stage Mr Patijn visited the national
capitals and his studies led him to formulate certain
basic orientations. It was agreed that the
distribution of seats should be reviewed and based on
certain objective criteria; that a deadline should be
fixed - 1980 was first proposed; that there should be
no transitional period; that the electoral system and a
maximum of other details should be settled at a
national level. The requirement of a 'uniform system'
would be met by laying down that elections were to be
by direct, universal suffrage with a secret ballot.
The opinion of the legal affairs committee supported
this approach.

The Political Committee imposed on Mr Patijn a
parliament of 550 seats. The main debate in plenary
session was on this issue and on the double mandate,
which the original report sought to phase out.
Proposals on seats varied from the 550 proposed to 355
(Legal Committee), 382 (Lord Rheay, UK conservative),
198 (Mr Nyborg, Danish EPD). The Legal Committee
proposal was accepted.(16)

The convention adopted on 15 January 1975 thus
provided for a parliament of 355 members, with 67 for
the United Kingdom, a voluntary double mandate and
elections to be held at a common date or period in
accordance with nationally fixed electoral laws. The
original proposal had been for the first election to be
in 1980, though Mr Peter Kirk as he then was, had
suggested 1982 as more realistic. However, the Paris
summit of 9 and 10 December had favoured 1978 as a date
and Parliament could easily accept this new earlier
date.

In the meantime there had been considerable progress.
On the face of it, when Mr Patijn was appointed in
1973, circumstances can hardly have seemed less
favourable for the adoption of a convention. Mr
Pompidou was still in power; France had been joined by
two new 'institutional sceptics' - Britain and Denmark.
The Community was soon to face the full blast of
economic crisis and renegotiation. However, the

election of Mr Giscard d'Estaing was to create a major change in French policy. Agreement to direct elections - but not on major extensions in Parliament's powers was to be the main achievement of a European summit in Paris in December 1974. Both Britain and Denmark reserved their position. Britain, and this is important, only reserved her position on the grounds that renegotiation was in progress and that the issue of membership had yet to be put to the British people.(17)

It was touch and go whether the momentum of the Paris summit could be kept up in the face of the major difficulties facing the Community. However, the fact that over the period from January 1975 the Council presidency was successively held by Ireland, Italy, Luxemburg and the Netherlands, all extremely favourable to the project, was advantageous.

At each successive summit, Dublin, Brussels and finally in Rome in December 1975 the decision became firmer and in Rome the European Council agreed unanimously to hold elections in May or June 1978. The British reservation of Paris 1974 was lifted and the Danish Prime Minister, with the backing of the Danish Parliament, redefined the Danish position. Denmark accepted direct elections provided Denmark could hold its election on a separate day to coincide with a Folketing election and could require that only members of the Folketing could be elected. This was agreed by the other governments.

There was no text of the convention agreed, nor was the number and distribution of seats fixed. All that was clear was that the European Parliament's convention was no more than a basis for discussion. When the Italian Government assumed the presidency in July 1975, a senior foreign office official was seconded to preside over an ad hoc working group which was to work on the details and report to the Council and then to the European Council. This group made good progress, but was unable to solve the issue of the number of seats.

The project ran into opposition on grounds of principle both in Britain and France, but in addition opponents raised the problem of national representation. Scotland would have to have a level of representation not far behind that of Ireland and Denmark. Both Ireland and Denmark insisted on retaining roughly their present degree of representation at least proportionately. Mr Fitzgerald (Irish Foreign Minister) pledged the Irish Government to this demand. Over the first six months of 1976 numerous plans were put forward and one European council failed to reach any agreement. The position of the British Government, favouring more seats than the European Parliament's proposal was supported by the first report of the select committee. At the July European Council in Brussels agreement was reached on a parliament of 410 members, each of the larger member states having 81 seats. Legal difficulties and the fact that France could only accept an act based on reciprocity in order to avoid the necessity of a constitutional amendment delayed the signature until 20 September 1976 and led to significant last minute changes in the text. Instead of exceptions for states which could not hold elections in 1978, it was agreed to fix no date in the Act itself and simply include the date as a decision of the Council. In this way, the obligations of each state became identical. A hard line Gaullist argument was thus hopefully undercut; however, it could lead to the risk that elections would be put off until a later date in all member states − the convoy so to speak proceeding at the pace of the slowest.(18)

Not inconsiderable difficulties remained to be overcome: ratification of the Act; passing electoral laws and the necessary administrative and political organisation of the elections. Each aspect will be examined in turn, with particular emphasis on those countries where problems still exist.

In Ireland, Luxemburg, Germany and the Netherlands no particular political problem has arisen in respect of implementation of direct elections. The technical

problems likewise seem fairly limited. In the
Netherlands a single national constituency is likely
to be chosen although the Prime Minister has raised the
possibility of multi-member districts or even some
version of the British system.(19) In Italy, the
problem is how to ensure at least some representation
for small and medium sized parties. One proposal from
the Secretary General of the Chamber is for nine
regional multi-member constituencies.(20) In Germany,
work on an electoral law is well advanced, and several
Länder have appointed senior officials who are to be
responsible for the preparation of elections. The
particular status of Berlin has been taken account of
in that a number of members of the German delegation
will be nominated by the Berlin Parliament. In
Ireland, there is some debate about the type of
constituencies to use. The government appears to
favour four multi-member constituencies electing 5, 4
or 3 members each.(21) These countries are using their
national electoral systems virtually unmodified.

Belgium faced a serious political problem in
implementing the Act of 20 September. All the main
political parties wholeheartedly support the principle
of direct elections, but the issue was inextricably
bound up with the central political issue in Belgium:
regionalisation (the Belgian equivalent of devolution).
The central issue has always been the position of
Brussels; was it or was it not a separate third region
in its own right? The Flemish parties have always
categorically denied Brussels such a status, whereas
the Francophone parties have insisted that Brussels
should have full regional status. The allocation of
the 24 Belgian seats in the directly elected European
Parliament ran into a parallel difficulty. How many
members would be elected and in what constituencies?
No party was prepared to concede a principle in respect
of European elections which could afterwards be used
against it in the domestic debate.

Earlier the Nothomb-Chabert bill for the direct
election of the Belgian delegation on a unilateral
basis had become bogged down in the Interior Committee

of the Chamber on precisely these grounds.

No one wanted to hold up a solution, but in late 1976
no immediate compromise was in sight unless there were
to be an agreement on regionalisation. Various schemes
were on the table. Prime Minister Tindemans proposed
a national list system; Mr Michel (former Interior
Minister) proposed three constituencies and the authors
of a paper(22) presented to the Liege Colloquium on
Direct Elections using groups of provinces. This
ingenious scheme would have failed, as did the
Tindemans and Michel schemes, to solve the difficulty
posed by Brussels. This was the more so in that they
proposed to use the Province of Brabant as a
constituency. Brabant includes Brussels-Capital and
much Flemish territory around Brussels.

In the event the problem neatly solved itself in the
wake of the dramatic Egmont Pact which paved the way
for the formation of the five party coalition
government in May 1977. This government includes the
Flemish and Walloon linguistic parties. This pact,
made possible by their gains in the April elections the
tactical acumen of Mr Tindemans and the Socialist
leaders, represented at long last a broad agreement on
the creation of regional authorities with wide powers.
The Government Agreement could also, by the same token,
provide an agreed solution to the allocation of the 24
Belgian seats. There are to be two constituencies: a
Flemish constituency electing 13 members and a Walloon
constituency electing 11 members. In Brussels and the
so called 'peripheral' Communes voters will be able to
opt for either list. Brussels voters will thus be able
to vote for the linguistic list of their choice, but
the Francophone/Flemish balance will remain fixed.

In Denmark the problems are almost entirely political
Denmark together with Britain has never shown the
marked popular enthusiasm for direct elections which
can be measured in the old six. It should be
remembered that the 'contract' under which Denmark
voted in October 1972 to enter the EEC was a
politically restrictive one.(23) The electorate was

promised that the EEC was almost entirely an economic
association and that the supra-national institutional
aspects would remain frozen at their present level. In
this manner, the degree of sovereignty given up was
tightly circumscribed. The anti-EEC forces which are
still well organised in the people's movement against
the EEC which is an umbrella group and in their
individual parties and organisations, have sought to
ensure respect for these limitations. They oppose
evasion of the veto power in the Council, direct
elections on a European Union. Most views were well
expressed in a recent article in Politiken by Jens
Maigaard(24) the European affairs spokesman of the
socialist people's party, in some ways the most
'constructive' of the anti-EEC parties and groups.
Here he argues that direct elections will inevitably
lead to greater integration and will upset the balance
of power between the institutions on which Danish
membership was based. He considers that the assurances
that no change in Parliament's powers is involved is
vain. For him, though admitting that the principle of
direct elections is in the Rome Treaty, the move to
direct elections should arise out of a genuine need for
them which he cannot detect in Denmark or in most of
the other member states. Such views are representative
of a wide range of broadly anti-EEC opinion including a
number of social democrats and radicals.

The Danish Government has, it would seem, under
pressure from its partners to accept direct elections,
sought to find a means of limiting their impact in
Denmark, avoiding conflict between Danish MEPs and
national MPs and finding a formula which would not
split the social democratic party. This formula was
the option for Denmark to hold elections on a separate
day, to coincide with Folketing elections (at least for
the first election) and to impose a compulsory 'double
mandate' in that only MFs could be elected MEPs. In
December 1975 the government obtained support for its
policy in a resolution passed with 29 voting against
and 10 abstentions. It has become clear both in the
course of this debate(25) and in subsequent discussions
in the Market Relations Committee that Parliament may

decline to take up the option which the social democratic (minority) government has obtained for it. (26) It would seem that the liberal, conservative, radical and progress parties at least accept neither reservation and that the SF may not accept combining the European elections with Folketing elections. Politically it is clear that combined elections would strengthen the tendency of anti-EEC social democrats to vote a straight party ticket which they might not do for a European election.

The government put several options in front of the Market Relations Committee: bills with and without the two reserves; a single national constituency or up to three constituencies (Copenhagen, Jutland and the Islands) each electing the appropriate number of members by the form of PR used in national elections. After discussions the government abandoned its reserves which were not included in the bill presented to the Folketing in October 1977 and passed in December.

Paradoxically, France was the first member state to complete all necessary domestic procedures for holding direct elections, whereas it had initially seemed likely to be the main obstacle. Domestic politics took a hand and achieved this dramatic result through a constitutional sleight of hand.

The debate on direct elections became enmeshed in a whole range of domestic issues: the increasing presidentialism of the régime; relations within the Presidential majority; relations within the Union of the Left; the personal ambitions and animosities of MM Barre, Chirac and Giscard d'Estaing.

The opposition to the project came both from the traditional wing of the RPR and from the communists. The danger was that concern for left wing unity would cause the socialists to decline to 'rescue' the President of the Republic's personal project or for the left to refind its unity in abstention. In either of these cases there would have been no parliamentary majority for direct elections.

The attitude of the communist party started out as totally negative.

Already in the European Parliament in January 1975, the French communists differed from their Italian colleagues in voting against direct elections. Each successive step towards direct elections has been condemned by the PCF. Commenting on the Rome summit, Mr Kanapa, member of the central committee of the PCF called direct elections:

'An alibi for democracy and an abandonment of national sovereignty, a monstrous plan against French sovereignty; German and other deputies will be able to impose their diktat on the French...' (27)

General Secretary Georges Marchais has called direct elections 'a crime against the French people'.

The French Socialist Party has by tradition favoured direct elections, but has in more recent years been forced to take account both the attitude of the PCF and of its own majority faction (the CERES – about 24 per cent of the delegate vote at the Pau (1975) and Nantes (1977) Congresses). Its position is based on the Common Programme which speaks of 'democratising' the EEC institutions and on the Resolution of the Bagnolet Congress (1973) devoted to Europe which supports direct elections under certain conditions.(28) It is among other things in the interpretation of these conditions that the 'Mitterandist' majority and CERES differ. For the CERES direct elections would impede the application of the Common Programme unless significant progress towards a socialist transformation had already been made.(29) The party as a whole also feared a new attempt to divide the left on Europe as had President Pompidou with his 1972 European Referendum. It is noticeable that the PS kept a low profile on this issue which disappointed some. With hindsight their low key approach seems to have paid off, especially when coupled with posing conditions to the government which had to be accepted. These were:

some form of proportional representation; no domestic
political manoeuvres. This policy enabled the PS to
mount a major, unpublicised effort or persuasion
towards their communist allies. This did not prevent
the party speaking out strongly and positively for
direct elections when this was possible. Both Mr
Mitterand and Martinet (member of the national
secretariat) spoke out firmly. In the National
Assembly debate on the bill, the socialist spokesman
J-P Cot emphasised the positive aspects of direct
elections - the opportunities which they offered to the
left.

Mr Mitterand, speaking to the Gauche européenne in
March 1976 declared 'we want direct elections not
merely for legal reasons, but because they meet a
political goal for us'. Mr Martinet (National
Secretary) in an interview to the ANSA Agency in
Rome has condemned the PCF attitude which he considers
'retrograde' with respect to the common programme of
the left signed in 1972. Both socialist leaders
referred to the danger of a new referendum splitting up
the left and Mr Martinet, speaking as he was in Rome,
accused the PCF of hindering cooperation of socialist
and communist parties in Southern Europe and of seeking
'...a "historical compromise" not with christian
democrats favourable to Europe, but with Gaullist
nationalism opposed to Europe'.(30)

When the bill finally came before Parliament in June
1977 a number of events had modified the initial line-
up on the left. The rising fortunes of the left in the
Spring of 1977 made a rupture on this issue more and
more unthinkable. Under discreet socialist pressure
and with the need to update the 1972 Common Programme,
the PCF shifted their position from out and out
opposition to a more moderate one of readiness to
accept the decision of the French Parliament and
guarantees (offered by the President) that the European
Parliament's powers could not be expanded. On 17 March
1977 he dramatically stated: 'Were the law (on direct
elections) to impose on the French members the duty to
exercise their powers within the strict limits of the

present Rome Treaties, we would be prepared to discuss the matter.' This was a considerable and positive step which was ultimately of great importance.

The left had always been able to derive comfort from the fact that whatever its own difficulties, those of the Presidential majority were at least as great. The issue was just as delicate for the President.

Soon after the Rome summit, two leading Gaullist figures, Mr Debré(31) and Mr Sanguinetti(32) wrote articles in Le Monde opposing direct elections on the grounds that they were an abandonment of the historical Gaullist doctrine of national sovereignty and a Europe built on 'les réalites nationales'. Mr Debré immediately recalls the European Defence Community – rejected in 1954 by the National Assembly, mainly as a result of a Gaullist-communist alliance. He argues that the convention presupposes a revision of the constitution or a referendum under article 11. For him once elected the European Parliament must increase its powers and undermine the independence of France. Mr Sanguinetti's arguments are similar. He says that 'any elected assembly will be sovereign....at a stroke we would move a Federal Europe'. Unlike some opponents of supra-nationality he does not remain passive and defensive in seeking maintenance of the status quo of national sovereignty. He calls the idea of national independence 'revolutionary' and unrelated to 'nationalism'. He conjures up the idea of a 'new battle of resistance and liberation' always a potent rallying cry in France and one which would as in the war find Gaullists and communists together. As if to confirm Mr Martinet's observation about a different 'historic' compromise, Mr Sanguinetti stated in an interview in the Nouvel Observateur(33) 'I accept the communists as objective allies; what's more I respect them and I am glad to see them rediscover, however late, the virtues of Gaullism'.

In a number of statements Mr Marchais has been far from reciprocating this admiration, even if he has claimed some Gaullist ideas.

In October 1976 Mr Debré formed a Comité pour l'Unité et l'Indépendance de la France which would organise opposition to direct elections. In his speech to UDR Assembly of the Indre-et-Loir, he recalled the EDC and how once again France faced 'an offensive of supra-nationality'.(34) The current Secretary General of the UDR, Mr Yves Guéna, has said: 'If the powers of that Assembly were in the end to come out reinforced, we could only condemn the slide towards supra-nationality'.(35)

Official reaction in the majority has been very prudent. The cabinet unanimously approved the decision reached at the Brussels summit of 12-13 July 1976, but the UDR ministers including Mr Chirac then their prime minister, underlined that the agreement concerned '... the composition of the Assembly and not its powers'.

The chairman of the UDR Parliamentary Group, Mr Claude Labbé, has mainly been concerned to avoid a split in the party on this issue. On 15 March 1976, the executive of the UDR passed a motion which underlined 'the evident dangers of the move to direct elections....such as a reopening of the old dispute on supra-nationality'. The executive decided to reserve its position.(36)

Even Mr Lecannuet, centriste and opponent of General de Gaulle in the 1965 presidential election underlined, before the senate on 16 December 1975, that the loss of sovereignty would be strictly limited.

President Giscard himself was of course to espouse a 'limited' interpretation of the move towards direct elections. He offered the special clause in the bill (later adopted) which states that major increases in powers for the European Parliament would require approval, in France, by the procedure for revising the Constitution. He was subsequently to claim in his Carpentras Speech of July 1977 that it was 'the final stone in the Community edifice; a logical and necessary reform'.(37)

By the time the bill was tabled, the waters appeared to be calmer in the Presidential majority and the bill seemed assured a relatively easy passage. This was not least due to the proposal of the President for the 'special clause' which had been enough to accelerate the shift in the PCF position and seemed likely to placate all but a hard core of 30-40 RPR deputies around Mr Debré.

The apparently technical question of the choice of electoral system raised political problems which timely government concessions solved.

Since the legislative elections of 1973, it has been very clear that the present two ballot system in single member constituencies and the present electoral boundaries favour the Presidential majority and more specially the UDR. The left would prefer proportional representation; some non-UDR leaders in the majority might be inclined the same way. However, the UDR was clearly opposed to any form of PR.(38)

At the same time, the doyen of French political scientists, Mr Georges Vedel, has argued that the 81 French MEPs will still be representatives of France; quasi-ambassadors and as such representative of the whole nation and never a part of it much less of a department, province or region.(39) His logic would impose a pure national list system.

This view gained much ground and in fact became a firm demand of the left. Although M Barre had, in October 1976, been unable to indicate any government position on the electoral system, in late January 1977 the Foreign Minister was to announce that the government would opt for a simple national list system. This was acceptable to all and was eventually passed into law.

The constitutional argument too, was undercut by the ruling of the Constitutional Council of 31 December 1976 that the Act of 20 September could constitutionally be ratified.

The victory of Mr Chirac in the Paris Municipal elections in March 1977 seemed to open a period, if not of harmony, at least of truce in the majority.

All these developments - those in the majority and those on the left - lulled the political world into a false and premature sense of security which left it unprepared for the RPR's thunderbolt. They reckoned without Jacques Chirac's preference for the dramatic and unpredictable. Faced with divisions in his RPR parliamentary group, exacerbated by tensions about forthcoming nominations for the parliamentary elections, he had to find a formula which could unite the group. This formula was one of open confrontation with the President. The RPR decided, prior to the 15-17 June debate on the government's bill to propose, under rule 127 of Assembly's standing orders, the adjournment of the debate until the next parliamentary session.

This dramatic move could, as indicative votes in the Assembly's Foreign Affairs Committee showed, have torpedoed the bill (RPR for the adjournment, centrists and republicans against but outvoted, the left abstaining). The Cabinet could not ignore the challenge, nor the danger. It invoked the special procedure of article 49(3) of the 1958 Constitution. Under this provision, the government may 'pledge its responsibility' on a bill. Unless a motion of censure is then passed against the government within 48 hours, the bill is passed automatically without debate or parliamentary consideration, as it stands. The RPR were unwilling to provoke a major political crisis and an early election and so backed down. Under these conditions no censure motion was tabled and the bill passed on 17 June 1977.

Under these conditions, the bill easily passed in the Senate early the next week. The bill fixing the electoral system and procedures likewise passed the National Assembly on 21 June and the Senate on 23 June without major difficulties.

Britain then became the member state most likely to hold up direct elections beyond the May/June 1978 target, but it should be said in fairness that the difficulties facing the Labour Government in early 1977 were both real and substantial. Furthermore, all British statesmen had since 1974 been at pains to point these difficulties out to their continental colleagues and had clearly underlined that the target of May/June 1978 might not be possible for Britain.

Throughout the debate in Britain a number of themes have been recurrent: the political debate within the Labour Party about the future of the Community; the choice of electoral system and the increasing weakness of the government and its consequent inability to impose any solution on the House of Commons in this or indeed any other matter. Its ability to carry a united cabinet or parliamentary party has even come into doubt. Under these conditions the issue became fraught with danger for the government which had to move slowly and tread warily.

The same issues have arisen as in France and Denmark, but in a manner adapted to the style of British political debate. The issues have been predominantly political, but other questions such as the distribution of the 81 seats between the constituent parts of the United Kingdom (Wales, Scotland and N. Ireland) and the electoral system have also been important in the debate. Since Britain has no written constitution, the issue of constitutionality has not come up in the same way, but the nature and extent of our obligation to accept direct elections under section 138(3) of the Rome Treaty has been raised by both sides.

In April 1969, the joint declaration of the British and Italian governments expressed support for direct elections; however, the issue was at that time hypothetical. As we have seen, neither The Hague (1969) or Paris (1972) summit conferences gave serious consideration to direct elections. The issue was not discussed in the enlargement negotiations nor to any real extent in the 'Great Debate' in Britain. In the

71

first year of British membership, with the Labour Party hostile, no institutional initiative could have been contemplated; even if it had come forward from other member states. At that time three member states were completely either unable or unwilling to consider direct elections. In the work of the political committee which began in earnest in the Autumn of 1973, Mr Kirk, as he then was, continually cautioned prudence in the matter. As late as February 1975 he was saying: 'I am enough of a sceptic to believe that 1978 is probably a rather optimistic date'.

During the renegotiation and referendum period from February 1974 until June 1975 the question of direct elections was not the subject of debate in Britain. At the Paris summit of 1974 Mr Wilson reserved the British position. That reservation was, unlike the Danish reservation, limited in time by reference to the impossibility of accepting direct elections until after the British people had accepted continued British membership of the EEC. By inference at least - and this is important in discussion of whether the position on direct elections was made clear before the referendum - it should have been clear that the British Government was in principle prepared to accept direct elections as early as December 1974, subject naturally to continued British membership of the Community.

Direct elections were not discussed greatly in the referendum campaign itself. Even in longer or more reflective articles or speeches on the future of Europe, the subject was barely mentioned and certainly not placed in the forefront of concern. However, it would be wrong to say that the subject was never mentioned at all; it would also be wrong to say that the pro-market forces did not indicate their support for the idea. They did not place great weight upon it. It was mostly the youth movements affiliated to Britain in Europe, who had an ambiguous relationship with the mother organisation precisely on the grounds of their insistence on mentioning the wider political aspects of the Community. For example, one press conference of Britain in Europe was given over to these movements, which declared: 'It must be a democratic Europe, with power vested in a directly elected parliament, such elections taking place in 1978 at the latest'. Mr Jeremy Thorpe, liberal leader, also expressed the same general line in a more restrained way:

> 'We have indicated that we want direct elections to the European Parliament by 1978 and a greater degree of integration of monetary, foreign and defence policies in Europe. In readiness for direct elections we are forming a European Liberal Party with our colleagues in the eight other countries and we have every hope of campaigning on a joint liberal manifesto in 1978.'(40)

However, he could hardly have been more explicit. At the last press conference of Britain in Europe before polling day its principal leaders, Mr Roy Jenkins, Mr Edward Heath and Mr Jeremy Thorpe, all declared their support for direct elections.(41)

It was only after the referendum, as the government began slowly to move towards acceptance of direct elections, that a debate on the issue got under way. This debate recreated more or less the battle lines of the referendum, with rather fewer conservative opponents of direct elections than of market membership.

On the 4 December 1975 Mr Wilson told the House of Commons, that 'I made it clear that we accept in principle the commitment to direct elections. This issue was decided by the referendum; article 138(3) of the Treaty of Rome is mandatory. But I added that we require a further period for consultations with political parties in this House and for consideration of the matter by Parliament before we could adopt a final position about holding direct elections ourselves as early as 1978.'(42)

Mr Hattersley, then Minister of State at the Foreign Office, speaking on the same day also told the Commons:

'If all goes well in time for an election in 1978,
then we can follow our partners. If we can not,
and here I can only repeat those doubts I expressed
in question time last week, we shall hold elections
properly even if later. I hope that our position
is understood by our partners as proof that we only
make promises which we can keep.'(43)

This has been the position of the government
throughout and it has been reiterated frequently in
question time: the insistence on the 'mandatory'
quality of article 138(3) and the fact that the
referendum had decided the issue of principle, but that
honesty dictated a prudent position on the realism of
1978 as an election date.

Almost every point of this position has been
contested by opponents of direct elections. Mr Bryan
Gould, MP, and Mr Nigel Spearing, MP, issued a
statement contesting the mandatory character of article
138(3). However, on 12 December 1975, in reply to a
letter from Mr Dickson Mabon, MP, Mr Wilson indicated
his belief that the 1978 date could be kept. Others
have argued that this early a date was unrealistic.

It was in the two day House of Commons debate on 29
and 30 March 1976 on the Government's Green Paper (Cmnd
6399)(44) that the full range of views came to be
expressed; spokesmen of all parties represented in the
Commons, as well as strong labour direct elections
supporters (John Roper-Farnworth, Dickson Mabon, Port
Glasgow) labour opponents of direct elections (Nigel
Spearing - Newnham SE, John Mendolsohn - Poplar),
conservative opponents of direct elections (Niel Marten
- Banbury, Roger Moate - Faversham).

Michael Stewart set the tone for the supporters of
direct elections when he said: 'that issue was settled
by the referendum'.(45) On the other side of the
argument, Niel Marten declared, 'I am against direct
elections, I always have been....I am against direct
elections because they will lead to a federal Europe.
Until we know the powers, we should not accept direct

elections'.(46)   From the Labour side of the House, Mr
Barnet asked, 'at whose expense will the Assembly gain
power?   They will have the effect of increasing the
authority of the Commission at the expense of the
Council.'(47)   For the Scottish National Party Mrs
Ewing said, 'I do not see how many people could
disagree with a step towards greater democracy.'(48)
In the European Parliament debate in September, she
went even further and said, 'I support direct
elections, even if Scotland does only get eight seats.'
(49)   Dafydd Wigley for Plaid Cymry declared that 'the
proposals for direct elections rekindle some of the
fears of last June....they are at the very least a
small step towards a Eurostate.'(50)   As might have
been expected, Mr Enoch Powell for the Ulster Unionists
placed the matter on a high plane; what was at stake he
said was '- the political independence of this country
and the political power of this House.'(51)   The issue
of the electoral system was also well to the fore.   Mrs
Ewing and Dafydd Wigley indicated a preference for the
alternative vote in single member constituencies
whereas David Steel (Roxburgh, Selkirk and Peebles -
liberal), while indicating strong support for direct
elections, devoted most of his speech to attacking the
first past the post system and proposing the use of
STV.   Numerous other speakers, including Mr Callaghan
and Mr Roy Jenkins and Mr Maudling appeared to rule out
any change in the electoral system.   Only Mr Barnet
expressed any support for finding a method which would
ensure liberal representation in the European
Parliament.

The party conferences of all three major parties
discussed the issue of direct elections in 1976 and
established or confirmed basic positions.   The Liberal
Party Conference at Llandudno strongly reiterated long
standing Liberal support.   There were though divisions
about tactics.   The Young Liberals and others such as
Christopher Mayhew (prospective candidate for Bath)
took up a more hard line position seeking to commit the
Party either to boycott or disrupt first past the post
European elections.   All these hesitations and
divisions were swept away in the new situation created

after March 1977 when the government's minority status led to the conclusion of the 'Lib-Lab' Pact. The Liberals were then able to impose the early introduction of legislation, as promised in the 1976 Queen's Speech and favourable consideration of the Liberal's views on PR. The Liberals then supported the bill on second reading.

The Conservative Conference in Brighton gave 'full hearted consent' to direct elections. The document The Right Way Forward gave enthusiastic support for direct elections and for the creation of a centre right alliance to counter socialism at the European level. All the same, doubts persisted about the strength of Mrs Thatcher's commitment and above all about her willingness to put the European cause above the narrowest party advantage. Could Conservative support be relied on for the second reading and subsequent procedural motions? In particular, when it became clear that the government would propose a regional list system, there was concern about Conservative negative attitudes. Mrs Thatcher's Rome speech in which she declared 'We are the European Party in Parliament and in the Country' dispelled these doubts. So it was that on 6 July all but fifteen Conservative MPs followed the party line and voted to give the bill a second reading.

As for the Labour Party, the situation is more complicated. In January 1976 the NEC passed the following motion:

> 'That the NEC request the Labour Government not to commit the UK to a European Parliament until the NEC and the Labour Party conference have had time to discuss the important implications.'(52)

In its evidence to the select committee the party reiterated this basic reserve, but addressed itself to some technical aspects which arose in part out of a study conducted by the party's organisation committee. Here it proposed that the election should coincide with a British parliamentary election in order to ensure higher turnout. The party itself received

76

evidence from a number of quarters including the Labour Committee for Europe and the Labour Safeguards Committee. In July 1976, in preparation for party conference the NEC took the unusual step of drawing up a document putting forward both sides of the case and simply indicating that the NEC had accepted the case against direct elections.(53)

After an at times passionate debate, conference on 29 September 1976 endorsed the NEC position in a card vote by 4,016,000 to 2,264,000. At the same time a motion condemning direct elections as a step towards a 'European superstate' was passed and one urging the party to prepare for direct elections in cooperation with other socialist parties was defeated. From the NEC document, from Mr Mikardo's reply to the debate on behalf of the NEC and from individual delegate speeches the arguments on each side appear to have been the following:

FOR DIRECT ELECTIONS

1.   Direct elections represent an elementary democratic step in the development of the Community which will enable the hitherto excessively bureaucratic machinery to be brought gradually under democratic control.
2.   Direct elections and the resulting politicisation alone will enable socialist objectives to be furthered in the Community.
3.   For a great democratic party such as Labour with its commitment to a gradualist parliamentary road to democratic socialism to reject direct elections would be a grave error.

These three points and particularly the last were put with great vigour and eloquence by John Cartwright, MP (Woolwich East), a member of the NEC and former anti-marketeer.(54)

4.   Fears about premature or automatic federalism are groundless especially in the present political climate.

1. Most of those opposing direct elections are 'unreconstructed anti-marketeers who do not desire to strengthen politically by giving an impression of democratic legitimacy, a capitalist organisation that they oppose and which in their view is in a state of disintegration.

2. To strengthen the EEC institutions is to make the achievement of a socialist Britain more difficult.

3. Direct elections will of themselves automatically lead us onto a 'slippery slope' towards federalism, thus undermining national and parliamentary sovereignty.

4. Cooperation with 'moderate' continental social democrats will lead to coalition politics and an edulcoration of Labour Party policy.

5. The inevitable low turnout, financial constraints and lack of clear cut issues will work against Lanour and lead to a Conservative landslide in direct elections.

6. Pressure for proportional representation for direct elections will have a precedent setting value for Westminster and Scottish and Welsh Assembly elections.

The larger trade unions were divided; the Engineering Union and the Transport and General were both opposed to direct elections and they alone cast almost 2,000,000 votes. On the other hand, the Municipal and General and USDAW (with 950,000 votes) were in favour.

It should be noted that the NEC statement did not obtain the necessary 2/3 majority to become binding party policy as specified in clause V(2) of the party constitution. Furthermore, the statement itself uses a very mild form of words in that it '...urges the government to bear in mind the decision of the annual conference of the Labour Party when it discusses the. question with its EEC partners.'

This is hardly a binding admonition to the government or the PLP, the more so since the act had already been signed on 20 September ending discussion of the matter at Community level. In order to remove all misunderstanding, Mr Crosland, Secretary of State, speaking the previous day at a socialist commentary meeting had declared, referring to the referendum:(56)

'that decision franked beyond further argument Britain's adherence to the Treaty of Rome. Article 138 of the Treaty of Rome clearly and unambiguously commits the Community to adopt a system of direct elections to the European Assembly. Any attempt by the British Government to wriggle out of that commitment would be infringing both the letter of the Treaty and the spirit of the referendum decision.' He went on to say: 'In these circumstances, for the government to go back on its word would be an act of bad faith, a betrayal of a decision democratically arrived at by the British people', and: 'I hope that conference will reject the advice of the NEC and support the decision taken by the government......But out of courtesy to conference, I must make one thing crystal clear. We regard the commitments we have made as binding ones. It therefore follows that, irrespective of the outcome of tomorrow's vote, the government will lay before Parliament the legislation needed to implement direct elections in Britain at the earliest practicable date.'

The government's resolve was thus 'crystal clear'. Since there could be no doubt of the existence of a majority for the legislation in Parliament, the only problem was then one of detail and timing.

Its own internal problems, which reached right into Cabinet itself, forced a prudent, temporising and consensus building approach on the government. It began the difficult task of gaining parliamentary support – not least within its own ranks – even before the formal signature of the act in September 1976.

As early as February 1976, the government issued a
Green Paper drawn up by the Home Office. Even at this
stage, the paper had certain 'white edges' in that
clear government views were expressed on certain
important issues such as the size of the Assembly ('an
assembly of about the size put forward in the
Assembly's own convention would be acceptable').(57)
A common election date or rather short period was
accepted in principle. In respect of matters for
decision by the British Parliament, a number of
preferences were expressed: use of the present
electoral system and an 'accelerated' boundaries
commission procedure were proposed.

The House of Commons debate in March seemed to
endorse the main suggestions. Nothing said by either
the Foreign and Commonwealth Secretary or by the Home
Secretary suggested any different conclusions. During
this debate Mr Callaghan announced the setting up of a
select committee which would be able to examine 'any
matter except the principle of direct elections'.

The debate held in the House of Lords also on 29
March covered substantially the same ground.(58) The
Lords, however, also had before them a report from
their select committee on the European communities
which had been able to examine the Green Paper and
even conduct a number of hearings. This report gave
particular attention to the matter of links between
MEPs and the British Parliament, examining ideas such
as making MEPs temporary Peers.(59)

It was not until six weeks later, on 12 and 17 May
that the Commons select committee was appointed with
the following composition:

```
     Labour (7) for direct elections:  Miss Boothroyd,
                                        Mr Cartwright
                                        Mr Hattersley
                                        Mr Horam
                          (chairman)    Mr Irving
            against direct elections:   Mr Gould
                                        Mr Kinnock
```

Conservatives (4)	Mr W. Clark
	Mr Fletcher
	Mr Hurd
	Sir Antony Royle
Liberal (1)	Mr Steel (later Mr Thorpe)
SNP (1)	Mr Reid

Total (13)

The committee was overwhelmingly favourable to direct elections and included no conservative present or past anti-marketeers. There were initially three Scottish and one Welsh member on the committee. Only one and perhaps two members could have been expected to approve any change in electoral system for direct elections. The committee was interesting in a number of ways. It was unusual in having a government minister as a member (Mr Hattersley) and in that its composition had been the subject of fierce debate. Attempts to vote Mr Niel Marten and Mr Douglas Jay onto the committee had failed.

The select committee received evidence from almost seventy organisations and individuals, including all the political parties, local authority organisations, government departments. Oral evidence was taken from departments, the speaker's council, the referendum counting officer, representatives of local authorities, of the boundaries commissions, the Liberal Party, the Labour Party.

Deliberations followed the lines that would be expected. Mr Gould and Mr Kinnock tabled amendments designed to call into question the realism of the 1978 target date. These amendments were lost. The Scottish members (joined by Mr Thorpe after he replaced Mr Steel) argued for ten members for Scotland. Mr George Reid alone tabled an amendment for sixteen members. Both these amendments were lost. Mr Thorpe tabled amendments (which were lost) seeking to leave open for the full House the question of the electoral system to be used.

The committee issued three reports.(60) The first (15 June) covered only matters for decision at European level. Its main recommendations were:

   a. for an assembly of 350-425 seats giving the UK enough seats to enable reasonable representation for Scotland and Wales;
   b. for elections in May/June 1978 at a period when no other elections are to be held, in a period fixed at the European level and common to all member states;
   c. for there to be no bar to joint membership of the European Parliament and the House of Commons on developed assemblies.

In its second report matters for decision by the United Kingdom were dealt with. The main recommendations were:

   a. a bill to be passed by February 1977, setting out the distribution of seats to the component parts of the United Kingdom, the electoral system and terms of reference for the boundaries commission;
   b. certain matters such as the franchise, eligibility etc. could even be embodied in a second later bill;
   c. the allocation of seats should be:
      England   66
      Scotland   8
      Wales   4
      Northern Ireland   3
                          ___

                           81
                          ___

The committee rejected arguments for greater Scottish or Welsh over-representation on parity with Ireland or Denmark.
   d. use of the normal first past the post electoral

system;
e. boundaries commissions should use an
'accelerated procedure' involving only one round of
appeals and hearings which could be concluded in
six months.

Under the timetable proposed by the select committee,
a bill introduced by the government in the Autumn 1976
should have become law in February 1977; thereupon the
boundaries commissions could embark upon their work,
grouping existing parliamentary constituencies to four
European Parliament constituencies. This procedure
would take from six to nine months.

The government did not seem to share the sense of
urgency(61) of the select committee. Matters were of
course not helped by the delay in signing the act.
Apart from the emphatic statements of Mr Crosland,
frequent reiteration by many ministers from the Prime
Minister downwards that the government would 'use its
best endeavours' to meet the May/June 1978 target and
the commitment in the 1976 Queen's Speech to legislate
in 'this session of Parliament' (i.e. before October
1977), the government was inactive. In retrospect this
temporising seems - at least temporarily - to have made
matters worse rather than better. The substantial
narrowing of the government's political and
parliamentary base, the virtual foreclosure of the
first past the post option if the May/June 1978
deadline was to be met and the reopening of the wider
debate about EEC membership inside the Labour Party all
occured after the bill should have become law on the
select committee's timetable!

However by March 1977 a number of converging
pressures were forcing some movement in the situation.

The NEC International and Organisation Committees
held to their view as endorsed by conference, but were
it seemed seeking some way out of an impasse which
could split the Party. In several meetings with
ministers they obtained no pledge from the government
not to proceed with legislation in this session.

Significantly, Mr Hayward warned the Party (at the Scottish Conference) that a collision with the government was in the making and should be avoided. He also opposed Mr Mikardo's view that Labour should refuse to fight direct elections.

There was a growing awareness that urgent action was needed lest Britain 'stand alone', but in an extremely unfavourable light. At the same time, backbench pressure on the government mounted through such initiatives as Mr Dykes' (Harrow East, conservative) private motion and Lord Banks' private member's bill in the Lords.

Mr Callaghan himself recognised the gravity of the situation, although he himself had never regarded the May/June 1978 target as an absolute obligation. Thus he told the Parliamentary Labour Party that 'the fact is that the government has to account for itself with other countries. If one country cannot have direct elections, then the other countries cannot have them either. This could have repercussions in other fields.'

On the other hand, the hard facts of by-election defeats such as Ashfield gave new credibility to the conclusions of a pamphlet by Michael Steed, Fair Election or Fiasco, in which he ably (from his Liberal political standpoint) demonstrates the danger for Labour of being reduced to a rump of five to eight seats - perhaps even less than the SNP - if the first past the post system was used. Even before the Lib-Lab Pact, Labour was showing an interest in PR. Home Secretary, Mervyn Rees said in March that 'the Cabinet has been considering very carefully all the problems arising from the use of our traditional electoral system in the European context. Different options have been examined, but none has been closed.' Here indeed were signs of movement.

Nonetheless, the Cabinet remained divided and all the government could do before the 1977 Easter recess was to issue a White Paper(62) with 'green edges' for

debate and discussion. The White Paper set out four
options: first past the post; the compulsory dual
mandate; the national list system; the regional list
system.

The increasing weakness of the government and the
conclusion of the Lib-Lab Pact on 23 March 1977
precipitated events. Hesitation on the need for an
early bill and at least a government recommendation in
favour of PR had to give way to action. The government
was now forced to act, but needed to avoid a conflict
in its own ranks and needed to dissociate the choice
of electoral system from the principle of direct
elections in order to maximise Conservative support.
Mrs Thatcher's Rome speech guaranteed Conservative
support for at least the second reading, but as was to
be shown later, not for PR.

The way out of the dilemma was the tried formula of
the referendum period in 1975; an agreement to
disagree both in the Cabinet and the PLP and reliance
on bipartisan support in the Commons. On 15 June the
Prime Minister told the PLP that all members including
Cabinet members would be permitted a free vote both on
second reading and the electoral system.(63)

Thus then the bill was published on 24 June 1977.
The bill is drafted with considerable ingenuity. In
the body of the bill, section 3(2) provides for the use
of the regional list system, but a schedule would
require the boundaries commissions to draw up 79 single
member constituencies in Scotland; England and Wales
and one three member constituency in Northern Ireland,
were Parliament to opt for the first past the post
system.(64)

The bill provides for Scotland (8 seats), Wales (4)
and Northern Ireland (3) to be regional constituencies.
Elsewhere, the planning regions are followed, except in
the South East where Greater London (10 seats) forms a
separate constituency. Parties would present lists
and individuals could also stand. Seats would be
allocated on the basis of the d'hondt largest remainder

rule. This system is considered slightly to favour the larger parties. Voters would vote for one candidate within the list. Seats would be allocated to a list and within it to those candidates who obtained the most votes.

The bill received a second reading on 6 July, by 394 votes to 147. 125 Labour MPs, including six Cabinet Ministers and 25 Junior Ministers voted against the bill. The bill then lapsed at the end of the session. The bill was rapidly reintroduced on 6 November and received its second reading on 24 November by 391 votes to 98. This time there was a two line-whip on the Labour side. Ministers were therefore only permitted to abstain and 32 did so. A further 60 Labour MPs voted against the bill. There was little new in the debate. Mr Enoch Powell repeated his warning that the bill was a slippery slope towards federalism. Douglas Jay reiterated his view that there was no obligation to introduce direct elections. For the government, the Home Office Minister, Mr Brynmor John repeated the government's minimalist view of direct elections. Of most interest was Mr Whitelaw's rejection of what he called 'the government's blackmail' on the electoral system. This pressure would not necessarily induce the Conservatives to support PR. The main battlegrounds were the allocation of seats to the constituent parts of the United Kingdom, on which the SNP and Plaid Cymru presented amendments; the choice of electoral system and the inclusion of a 'political' clause along French lines declaring limitations on the extension of the powers of the European Parliament. This last line of attack was foreshadowed in two articles in Labour Weekly by John Prescott (Hull East, labour). He accepts the inevitability of direct elections, but seeks both to defend the sovereignty of the British Parliament against encroachments and to develop a constructive future role for the European Parliament with strictly limited powers.

The parliamentary debates furnished little in the way of new arguments or surprises, but rather confirmed well known positions. As was expected, the House of

Commons rejected the PR system on 13 December 1977, by 319 votes to 222.

NOTES

(1)   See appendix, p.165.
(2)   L'Assemblée commune de la CECA, P.J.G. Kapteyn, Sijthoff 1962.
(3)   Kapteyn, op.cit. See also Resolution No.27 in Journal officiel of 11 December 1954.
(4)   Parlement Européen. Pour l'élection de P E ou suffrage universel direct, September 1969, pp.22-68.
(5)   For details of the convention see Parlement Européen, op.cit., pp.236-41.
(6)   Doc 47 presented by Mr Dehousse on Political Cooperation.
(7)   Doc 110 presented by Mr Pleven.
(8)   J.O. 63 of 20 April 1963.
(9)   J.O. 106 of 12 July 1963.
(10) J.O. No.C 41 of 1 April 1969.
(11) Document 686/69 AG 102.
(12) Communiqué final de la Conférence des chefs d'état et de gouvernement.
(13) For a short summary of these developments, see the explanatory statements to Mr Patijn's Report, Document 386/74.
(14) Patijn Report para 25.
(15) Patijn paras 26-7.
(16) European Parliament, debates 15 January 1975.
(17) See final communiqué paragraph.
(18) For the texts see appendix.
(19) Grondwet en Europese Verkiezingen, Mr Waanders, NRC Handelsblad, 23 July 1976, p.3.
(20) Article in 'Il Mondo', 25 August 1976, p.23.
(21) Direct to Europe, John Cooney in The Irish Times of 20 July 1976.
(22) Paper by Jean Beaufays and Henry Breux: l'Election du P E ou suffrage universel: quelques problèmes techniques à resonance politique, March 1976.
(23) See Scandinavian Referenda and EEC Entry, J. Fitzmaurice, European Review, Spring 1973 and J. Fitzmaurice, National Parliament and European Policy

Making: the Case of Denmark, in Parliamentary Affairs, vol.XXIV, no.3, Summer 1976, pp.284-6.
(24) Jens Maigaard: Politiken, 14 January 1976.
(25) Folketing Handlinger, December 1975.
(26) Berlingske Tidende, 17 July 1976, p.4.
(27) Agence Europe, 5 December 1975, p.3.
(28) Resolution of the Special Congress, held at Bagnolet, 15 December 1973.
(29) Motion no.2: 'Pour Appliquer le Programme commun: Unité, Autogestion, Indépendence', Ac and Annexe, in Le Poing et La Rose, no.62, June 1977.
(30) Interview in ANSA, 8 March 1976.
(31) Mr Debré: l'Aventure reccomence, Le Monde, 17 December 1975.
(32) A. Sanguinetti: La nouvelle résistance, Le Monde.
(33) Reported in Agence Europe, 10 March 1976.
(34) Le Monde, 9 October 1976.
(35) Le Quotidien de Paris, 27 September 1976, p.3.
(36) Agence Europe, 18 March 1976.
(37) Le Monde, July 1977, p.1.
(38) The Economist, 15 October 1976.
(39) Des Representants de la Republique, Maurice Duverger in Le Monde, 20 July 1976, p.1.
(40) The Times, 23 May 1975.
(41) The Times, 5 June 1975.
(42) The Times, 5 December 1975.
(43) Ibid.
(44) Cmnd 6399, Direct Elections to the European Assembly.
(45) House of Commons Debates, vol.908, no.79, 29 March 1976, col.928.
(46) HC debs. col.964.
(47) HC debs. col.976-7.
(48) HC debs. col.949.
(49) European Parliament, debates, 15 September 1976.
(50) HC debs. col.987.
(51) HC debs. col.1150.
(52) See NEC statement: Direct Elections, Arguments for and Against.
(53) See NEC statement.
(54) Report of the Seventy Fifth Annual Conference of the Labour Party, Afternoon Session 29 September 1976, pp.244-5.

(55) An example of these arguments can be found in a
note by Bryan Gould, MP in The Original Briefing, 29
September, p.5 (a Conference fringe publication) and
Reply to the debate on behalf of the NEC by Ian Mikardo
MP, Conference Report, pp.250-3.
(56) In Conference Commentary, 29 September 1976.
(57) Cmnd 6399, para 19.
(58) House of Lords, Official Report vol.369, no.53, 29
March 1976.
(59) 22nd Report of the Select Committee of the House
of Lords on the European Communities, Direct Elections
to the European Assembly.
(60) 1. First Report from the Select Committee on
         Direct Elections to the European Assembly (15
         June 1976).
      2. Second Report of the SC......(3 August 1976).
      3. Third Report of the SC.......(14 October and 9
         November 1976).
(61) The Third Report underlines the urgency of action
and deals with electoral procedures and voting
qualifications.
(62) Cmnd 6768: Direct Elections to the European
Assembly (April 1977), especially paras 8-24.
(63) The Times, 16 June 1977.
(64) The European Assembly Elections Bill, see
especially Sections 2,4, Schedules I and III.
(65) The Times, 7 July 1977.

4 European party cooperation and the accountability of MEPs

The holding of direct elections is a unique political event in that for the first time voters will be electing members to a parliamentary body outside their own state. This fact will impose new thinking on voters and on political parties, without which no modern election could have any meaning. It is the parties which present the citizen with a real choice between programmes, approaches and ideals. Parties attempt to place before the electors a range of measures and an 'image' which taken collectively add up to what the French call a <u>projet de société</u> - a view of how society should develop.

The key to voter interest and therefore to voter mobilisation for direct elections as well as to the possibility that the elected parliament will be able to claim a mandate to increase its powers, lies in effective party competition and confrontation. The point that the willingness of the political parties to participate fully in the elections will make or break the elections cannot be sufficiently underlined. If it is a physical fact that nature abhors a vacuum, it is almost as true that political parties abhor a power vacuum. Accordingly, it is to be expected that the political parties will, almost by instinct or by reflex, react to this new dimension to politics and seek to organise the elections in such a way as to impose their view of reality. Parties act both to occupy 'the high ground' and to bar the way to their opponents. All these forms of party activity have begun on the European level. Certainly the activity is uneven, as between the different parties and many questions still remain to be solved. However, it is assured that the parties will as far as circumstances

90

and available time and resources permit play their part in giving the first European elections the impact which its proponents wish it to have. This chapter will seek to analyse the nature and scope of such party activity.

European elections will, at least for the first election, very largely be nine national elections with a European dimension. With certain exceptions, which we shall examine, the organisation and political topography of the elections will be familiar to the voter. He will encounter candidates and campaigns from the political parties he knows on the national level, but seeking to present their own distinctive approach to European Community problems, perhaps in loose alliance with Community wide groupings of like-minded parties.

As we shall see, attempts to create new European parties from the base or even tightly structured confederal groupings, have been relatively unsuccessful, at least up to now. It is possible that the mere fact of elections will increase the impetus towards closer party integration, but for the moment it seems that existing national parties will form the basis of the campaign. It, therefore, follows that the question of party activity must be examined at two levels: the national level and the European level.

At the national level the first question must be whether the European election campaign will follow the traditional patterns of national party confrontation or whether modified patterns will occur. The likely outcome for the various member states would seem to be:

Traditional pattern: Belgium
                              Germany
                              Ireland
                              Luxemburg
                              United Kingdom

Modification possible: Denmark (depends on the
                                         electoral system)
                                France
                                Italy
                                Netherlands

In France alliances would only have been necessary if
the present two ballot electoral system was used.
These alliances might simply have been in the normal
majority (RPR, Giscardians, Centrists) v left (PSF, PCF,
Radicaux de gauche) pattern. However, since both blocs
contain wide, and developing divergences of opinion on
European issues, some different alliances, at least in
some constituencies might have been possible. The
choice of a national list system with a five per cent
threshold may force some smaller parties (e.g. MRG) to
seek joint lists with other parties.

In Holland and Italy the large number of parties
(Italy ten parties, Holland eleven parties) would make
adequate representation for them all impossible. As a
result some parties (such as the Liberals and
Republicans in Italy)(1) might join forces for European
elections and others (DS-70 in Holland) might not
contest European elections.

In Denmark much would depend on the electoral system
and of course the large number of parties is also a
factor. Since list alliances will be permitted, some
joint anti-EEC lists may be formed, even under the
umbrella of the People's Movement against EEC. Such a
list might win more seats than could the individual
anti-EEC parties which in terms of total vote could
only expect to win at the most two seats.

Some have argued that direct elections should not be
confined to the pre-existing parties or even groups of
parties, but that a larger role should be accorded to
independents or to candidates endorsed by non-party
organisations such as the European Movement, or by
umbrella organisations such as the Common Market
Safeguards Committee and new groups such as ecologists.
(2) The French and Germans have made explicit

reference to this possibility, but the five per cent threshold would probably prevent any members being elected. Mr Molenaar, the Chairman of the Dutch section of the European Movement has suggested the calling of a new European congress in The Hague to endorse candidates. It is not clear whether such an idea is limited to Dutch candidates or to 'good Europeans' among party candidates or seeks to nominate its own candidates. Until the referendum, with its non-party umbrella groups such ideas could hardly have been entertained in Britain; even now they must remain unlikely since the decision to put up and choose candidates would probably alienate members of some organisations and reduce their future ability to cooperate with political parties. Such candidates would be unlikely to be elected.

The attitude of organisations other than political parties can play an important role in mobilising opinion, in shaping the campaign, in giving the elections relevance and significance and in giving the Parliament substance and reality. The greatest compliment that could be paid the Parliament would be for interest groups to take it seriously.

It has to be said that up to now, interest groups and professional organisations have concentrated their attention on the Commission and on national governments. They have rarely considered contacts with Parliament to be important.(2a) There are exceptions; these are precisely in those areas where Parliament does in fact already have some power. For example, steel firms have been active in lobbying Parliament for reductions in the Coal Steel Community turnover levy, which is set by the Commission, but only after a concurring opinion from Parliament. Were Parliament to gain in power and importance, it is likely interest groups would attach greater importance to it.

Direct elections can change that situation in two ways. Firstly, direct elections offer the prospect of a stronger Parliament. More immediately, though, the campaign will provoke a debate about Europe, in which interest groups can intervene. It will offer them a platform or a peg on which to hang the issues which concern them. Some of these groups may organise parallel campaigns to force certain issues into the debate and to force parties and candidates to react to these issues. The campaign would then develop an issue orientation (employment, agricultural policy reform, policy towards the Third World) that it might otherwise lack.

One can give some examples of bodies which have already begun to make preparations for such activity.

The European Trade Union Conference (ETUC), in its statement on direct elections(2b) made its position clear. It supports direct elections, but regards neither them nor the Parliament as a substitute for its own activity. Accordingly, it proposes to organise its own parallel campaign to promote its own economic and social case:

> The Executive Committee of the European Trade Union Confederation considers this direct universal suffrage to be an important step inasmuch as it will bring about a more extensive and fundamental democratisation process, which the ETUC, moreover, has been demanding for some time. The trade union organisations have in fact repeatedly criticised the lack of democracy in the Community decision taking processes and have even come to wonder whether the extension of the Community powers of decision would not also bring the consolidation of Community democracy.

> The European Trade Union Confederation will use the electoral campaign to propagate its demands in this field. A detailed programme will be drawn up to this effect as soon as possible.

> The Executive Committee wishes to emphasise, however, that the democratisation process advocated by the trade unions will not attain its full value unless it is used to find a better means of meeting

the socio-economic aspirations of workers. The
trade unions will thus also make use of this
campaign to intensify their pressures favouring
more effective action (for example: action to
combat unemployment, to improve the living and
working conditions of workers, and to guarantee
the purchasing power of workers' incomes and social
benefits).

On no account will the trade union movement allow
this electoral campaign to be used to distract
workers from their problems and demands. On the
contrary, the European Trade Union Confederation
and its affiliated confederations in member states
of the European Economic Community will have to use
this campaign to confront the political parties and
candidates with their social and economic demands.

The International Coalition for Development Action,
(ICDA), a body coordinating national development action
and Third World oriented groups, has likewise taken the
view that the direct elections campaign could offer
them opportunities to sensitise public opinion to the
complex and politically difficult issues of development
policy. The Coalition has held a series of meetings to
consider what might be best form of coordinated action
and to encourage the national groups to undertake their
own campaigns.

Even where no question of new patterns of party
activity arise, parties will have to face a number of
organisational problems. Parties will have to decide
whether to use traditional procedures for the
nomination of candidates which might in some countries
(the UK) involve an almost completely decentralised
system and in others a largely centralised system.
National parties might wish to exercise some degree of
influence to ensure a balance of interest, age, sex and
experience among candidates in winnable seats or
positions on lists.(3)

In Britain the Conservative Party has already
received a large number of applications to stand as

candidates. A wide selection of people, including some MPs, has come forward. The Liberal, Labour and Scottish National Parties are less far advanced. The Conservatives intend to use a procedure similar to that applied for Westminster, with a panel setting candidates for an approved list, but with the final choice lying with the individual European constituency organisations.(4) Apart from a study by the Party's organisation committee, the Labour Party has done no work on this issue.(5)

Parties will also have to consider the nature of the campaign; will the campaign follow the normal pattern or will it be to a much greater extent a national media campaign?(6) The referendum has shown that such a media campaign can be effective, but that was in a campaign where no local issues would matter significantly and there were no individual 'marginal' constituencies. Certainly in constituencies of 500,000 votes the potential of regional radio and television will have to be mobilised and great reliance will have to be placed on national campaigns by party leaders and even by European figures from the different groupings organised at a European level.

As we shall see, European parties in the sense we know the party in national politics will not come about. Broad party groupings with a basic infrastructure, an outline platform and pledged to common action in the European Parliament will come. Adherence to such groups can give a greater sense of devotion and coherence to the campaigns of individual parties which would otherwise seem isolated and insignificant in a European context. Practical help in the form of leaders participating in meetings and broadcasts in other member states, distribution of a certain amount of common literature and the availability of European finance and(7) specialised research facilities (vital in dealing with an unfamiliar subject), could help national parties. These will nonetheless remain the masters of their own campaign.

It is at least possible, that even if the election is party dominated the campaign may as in the United States, be more individualistic than in national elections.(8) The candidate is elected not to sustain a government, but to put forward certain views, to be sensitive to regional opinion and only in a very general sense to carry through a party programme. This, coupled with the large electorates may make for more scope for individual stands and even deviance from party views. Each individual candidate will have to make it clear, within the general confines of party policy, what he expects to do if elected; what role he expects to play in the directly elected Parliament and how he intends to maintain contact with his constituents and with his political party.

If the regional list system proposed by the government is followed, voters must vote for an individual on the list. The number of individual votes will determine the order of election. Candidates will therefore to some extent be in competition with others on their list.

At the European level too party organisation is coming into being. It has long been considered that the political development of Europe could only come about if political parties organised themselves to take part in European politics. Whatever may be the theoretical justification for a 'common market of political parties',(9) the reality is that the Community has certainly not reached a stage of development where such creations would be possible.

European parties will then be something very different from the kind of parties that we know at the national level. The tightly knit organisation; the detailed and binding programme; the organic links between the parliamentary party and the mass party outside parliament and above all the common heritage of shared experience and shared political battles which gives a party its sense of cohesion, will be absent.

The experience of the political parties across

Europe, even those which share the bond of a common ideological background, has been very different; their concerns, as well as their structures and styles have grown out of different conditions and circumstances. German Christian Democrats can 'confront' socialism; Benelux Christian Democrats are usually in coalition with socialists. The German SPD's attitude to communism mirrors the problematic relation between the Federal Republic and the DDR. The French Socialist Party can only achieve power in an alliance with the strong French Communist Party. The nature of British socialism may or may not owe 'more to Methodism than to Marxism' but it is certainly sui generis.(10)

European elections are, also, a kind of 'partial election' in that the European Assembly is not omnipotent, indeed the Community itself is not omnipotent. As is well known, the Community only exercises certain powers in the fields of public policy covered by the Treaties setting up the communities. In this they will be similar to local government elections and to devolved assemblies, but will differ from national parliamentary elections. There will be no requirement for parties to put forward a comprehensive policy statement concerning all areas of policy. For example, divisive issues of an ethical or moral character which are not relevant to the EEC can be ignored. Emphasis should be on issues on which parties in the same 'political family' can agree. Issues chosen for a 'common platform' should be based on relevance to the Community and salience to the electorate. The common platform would take the form of an action programme which national parties could use in their national campaign. In the campaign itself the role of 'European parties' would probably be limited to acting as a clearing house for exchange of information, for provision of information, for exchange of speakers between fraternal parties and for the disbursement of Community funds which may be made available for campaign purposes.

Two meetings have been held between Mr Dröscher (chairman of the Confederation of Socialist Parties),

Mr Tindemans (European People's Party) and Mr Thorn (Federation of Liberal and Democratic Parties) at which the issues of finance, the role of the mass media in the campaign, the future legal status of European parties were explored.

European parties will, therefore, have a loose structure which might be compared to the structure of American political parties, which are in reality federations of state parties only assuming a national identity every four years at each Presidential election. Their platforms, too, will correspond more closely to the American style party platform than to a national programme or election manifestos.

What has been achieved up to now? Transnational party activity in the framework of international organisations has hitherto been limited and of only marginal importance to the participating national parties.(11) In transnational parliamentary bodies other than the European Parliament, cross-national political organisation and even activity has been weak and desultory. Political groups do exist in the Consultative Assembly(12) of the Council of Europe and in the Western European Union Assembly, but not in the Nordic Council.(13) The activity of these groups has not been very intense and has not led to the formation of any extra parliamentary organisations. Even in the relatively politically homogeneous environment formed by the members of the Nordic Council, no discernible cross national initiative has developed; national delegations as such have played a more significant role than parties.(14)

As we shall see in greater detail, the four major political families in Europe (Socialist, Christian Democrat, Liberal, Communist) all have created arrangements for party cooperation, in such bodies as the Socialist International, World Union of Christian Democrats (and its European regional organisation), the Liberal Internation and Communist world and regional conferences. However, such bodies have no decision making powers and serve mainly as platforms for periodic summit meetings of member parties' leaders. As such they generate useful mutual information and comparison of problems and situations, but no more.

It is only in the EEC framework where there has been any significant degree of transnational parliamentary activity. Even here it has been limited to the creation of groups in the European Parliament.(15) In reality these groups are independent both of their home parties who could not in any case exercise any collective control over them, and of the until now extremely weak transnational party organisations which are in any case politically and administratively dominated by the European Parliament groups with whom they often share a secretariat. This may have some advantages, but does limit them to somewhat 'irresponsible' (in a technical sense) pro-European pressure groups, and as such reduces their acceptability and influence. To really British minds at least such non-accountable, purely parliamentary groups could not be accepted as long term solutions. These groups have, it has been argued elsewhere, become effective in the limited context of the European Parliament. They are 'Fraktionen', to use the German term, or very similar to the combinations of 'independents' which under the French IVth Republic formed unstructured 'groupes parlementaires' without any mass party organisation. Even today in France such arrangements are not unknown: the National Assembly and Senate Groups are different; various 'centriste' National Assembly groups have at times been little more than subterfuges to get round the thirty member minimum for a group. Even the fédération de la gauche démocratique et socialiste (1967-69) was a classic 'groupe parlementaire' based on three independent components uncoordinated outside parliament. It may well be that the creation of such 'Fraktionen' is a stage towards the formation of more integrated parties, but certainly this has not as yet happened at the European level.

One evident reason for the difficulty in proceeding beyond this embryonic 'Fraktion' stage is, that in the

European Community context, the implications of such a development would be considerable and perhaps incalculable, going beyond what the large national political parties (Labour, Conservative, SPD, CDU) would be prepared to contemplate. They are only too well aware of these implications. Not least because those who favour party integration have spelled out these implications and have indeed espoused them eagerly as the very basis of their support for a 'common market of political parties'.(16) The first effort to create a common electoral programme (the so called Birkelbach Report) in 1962 was as now related directly to a drive towards European elections then thought to be imminent; it was in fact not related to any strengthening of European level socialist party organisation, which had weakly existed since 1957 in the liaison office of socialist parties in the EEC and in any case no other parties matched this socialist programme. In the later 1960s and early 1970s, party cooperation and indeed the creation of European parties was seen as not directly tied to and indeed independent from direct elections.

Supporters, both socialist and christian democrat, but mostly Dutch or Italian, of such ideas argued that the creation of European parties was a means of politicising the EEC and creating a counterweight to bureaucratic and technocratic integration whose social and political content was too limited. Direct elections were seen as supporting party integration and perhaps less important than such integration. At any rate this aim was to be pursued irrespective of whether direct elections could be achieved. Initiatives to this end by Mr Vredeling, Mr Mansholt, Mr Westerterp and Réné Montant were taken over and diluted or rejected by the existing party structures.(17) It was thereby confirmed that any development could only grow out of closer coordination of existing party activity, indeed out of confederal structures. European party construction could not bypass or undermine the established parties. Thus new or revitalised 'unions', 'confederations' or 'federations' have taken the existing parties as their basic building blocks and are

are directed more to the immediate issue of direct
elections than to the aim of bringing about a decisive
shift in European politics.

THE LEFT

a. The Communists

The international relations of communist parties have
always been strong, but until recently there has been
no regional organisation nor any regional conferences.
Even now, the communist parties have not established
any cooperation machinery covering the European
Community as such, although bilateral PCI-PCF
relations, as well as the newly established European
regional conferences have been to a large extent
dominated by Community and related issues. No European
communist organisation is contemplated in order to
fight direct elections.

This is not the place to relate the development of
communist positions on the Community in any detail. We
shall confine ourselves to the milestones along the
way.(18) After the abolition of the COMINFORM in 1956
there was no formal machinery for cooperation among CPs
except through periodic world conferences organised
under Soviet auspices.

The 1962 conference in Moscow was important in the
EEC context in that it saw the adoption of the thirty
two theses against capitalist integration in Western
Europe(19) which codified the positions communists had
taken already in national debates on both the ECSC, the
EDC and the EEC. These consecrated the view 1. that
the EEC was an economic arm of NATO and hence an
instrument of US hegemony, 2. that the EEC could not
increase prosperity, 3. that the EEC hindered the
achievement of socialism in its member states.(20)

Already, in the 1959 Regional Conference, the PCI had
tentatively begun a theoretical re-evaluation of the
EEC and the 1962 conference saw the first signs of

(open) Italian dissidence. Mr Longo had told the
Central Committee that 'the EEC has become a
determinant element in the Italian economic recovery'.
(21) In the period 1966-69 the CGIL and the PCI sought
and obtained representation in EEC institutions and
Amendola was able in November 1971 to inform the
Central Committee that 'a whole new field of initiative
and activity for communists has opened up'. The PCI
has played a constructive role in the European
Parliament and supports direct elections - and indeed
has done so for several years. The PCI made serious
attempts to define its European policy, for example
during the colloquium held in Rome in November 1971
under the title 'I communisti italiani e l'Europa'
which saw the presentation of reports on the main areas
of Community policy and an extremely open debate both
with foreign communists and Italian and foreign non-
communists.

The Brussels conference of Western European Communist
Parties saw a reaffirmation of the positive position of
the PCI on Europe by Secretary General Berlinguer and
Mr Amendola. The latter indicated that the PCI's goal
was 'the democratic transformation of the Community
from the inside'.(22)

In spite of the evident rapprochement between the PCI
and PCF strong differences remain with the PCF, as we
have seen opposed to supra-national institutions and
indeed to direct elections. Even here, the PCF has
recently moved closer to the PCI, abandoning its
opposition à outrance to direct elections. On economic
matters, there is a convergence of analysis but not of
policy prescription. The PCF favours the return to
national 'economic sovereignty' and nationalisation as
a reaction to monopolistic tendencies, whereas the PCI
favours countervailing Community level control.(23)

The main axis of the communist movement in Europe is
the PCI-PCF, who are the only parties with any
significant national position. Their cooperation is
all the more important in the absence of any formal
organisation at the European level.

As indicated, regional conferences have been held since 1959 (Geneva), in 1971 on multinationals and the most important in Brussels in 1974. At the end of that conference, Mr Marchais told the press: 'we exclude the idea of a simple decision centre for the European or world communist movement; the conference has created no secretariat nor any other common organisation at European level'.(24)

PCF-PCI 'summits' are, therefore, important in view of their dominance over the movement and since they alone can expect significant representation in the European Parliament. The 1966 San Remo summit and the Rome meeting of November 1975 led to a significant evolution in mutual understanding on the EEC; the PCF position will become even more delicate if the Union of the Left were to win power in France in 1978.

Enlargement of the Community to include Spain, Portugal or Greece, currently possible candidates for membership, would not increase relative communist support greatly, but in all three potential members, there would be some communists elected. There are four parties: the PCP (Portugal), the PCE (Spain) and the Interior Communist Party and the Hellenic Communist Party (KKE). The Spanish party and the Greek 'interior' party are on an Italian 'eurocommunist' line whereas the PCP and KKE are loyal to Moscow and to traditional communist policies and methods.(25)

b. The Socialists

Relations with communist parties have been a very contentious issue among socialist parties, especially between the SPD and the French party. This was evident at the Elsinore meeting of the Socialist International and Confederation Bureau. No prediction can be made at this stage about likely socialist-communist relations in an elected European Parliament. Certainly the threat of a 'popular front' evoked by CDU Secretary General Biedenkopf is probably not an immediate reality. The degree of cooperation is likely to depend on events in France and Italy.

The socialist parties have a long history of transnational cooperation, mostly on a somewhat pragmatic and informal basis. The Socialist International has a long history and held its first post war congress in Frankfurt in 1951. It currently has some thirty-three full member parties mostly from Western Europe and a number of observer parties. Of its fifteen million membership, some 50-60 per cent is located in Western Europe. In recent years meetings of its Bureau have tended to become informal summits of socialist leaders in the Community and EEC issues have dominated these meetings.(26)

There have also been attempts to create left wing European movements, transcending in some sense the national parties. The movement for the Socialist United States of Europe, launched by the ILP in 1947 soon became more pragmatic, changing its name to the Socialist Movement for the United States of Europe and cooperating with the much more broadly based European movement. It gave birth, in 1961, to the more structured European Left, which now has some ten national sections, holding periodic congresses. From the early days of the Community, a conference of the socialist parties of the European communities has existed (founded in 1957) and in 1958 a 'liaison office' was set up, changing its name in 1971 to the Office of the Social Democratic Parties in the European Community.

In prospect of direct elections the parties approved two policy programmes: the agricultural programme, adopted in April 1961 and the more general programme was adopted at the fifth congress, held in Paris from 5-6 November 1962. This programme contained chapters on European political structure, economic organisation, social policy, cultural activity and international law. There were as we know no direct elections and these programmes remained isolated efforts in this area.

In the period when direct elections were not in

prospect, other considerations, such as those outlined previously led figures such as Mr Mansholt, Mr Vredeling and Mr Montant to move in a new direction. (27) They were acutely aware that the 'intergovernmental' approach to party cooperation, leaving the existing party structures intact and laying no binding obligations on the national parties, had not made much progress. Accordingly, they sought to create the embryo of a new European party, which Mr Vredeling called the Progressive European Party. Its aim was to have a shock effect and hence create the conditions for cooperation hitherto lacking. An 'action committee for the formation of a European Socialist Party' was formed in 1968 and later became the committee for the creation of a Federation of European Socialist Parties, publishing its proposals in October 1973.

Such initiatives ran into a double opposition: that of the existing parties, and particularly the SPD and secondly from those who argued that such an initiative was meaningless until there existed a minimum quantum of power to be exercised at the European level, thus permitting the party to exercise the traditional function of a party.(28) In the face of this opposition, these initiatives were channeled back through the traditional party structure and only achieved minor success. The 1971 Brussels Congress of the Parties did adopt a very wide ranging and detailed programmatic declaration; the Dutch Labour Party Congress of the same year adopted a resolution calling for a special congress of the parties for the adoption of an emergency programme and an eventual 'federative partnership' between the parties. In 1972 the Office of Social Democratic Parties sent out a questionnaire to the member parties on this issue, leading in due course to the formation of the Confederation of Socialist Parties in the European Community in 1974.

This reorganisation provided for more regular congresses, to be held every two years. It also strengthened the Bureau which now meets at least four times each year and may issue recommendations to

member parties and statements on topical issues. The
congress may by two-thirds majority, on a unanimous
proposal from the Bureau, adopt decisions binding on
the member parties. The congress elects its president
and vice presidents for two years.(29) These are
currently Mr Wilhelm Dröscher (SPD) and Mr Sicco
Mansholt (PvdA), Mr Ivor Nørgaard (Social Demokratiet),
Mr Pontillon (PS).

The Confederation consists of ten parties (two
Italian parties) from all member states. The Labour
Party did not join the Confederation until early 1976
and had until then only occasionally sent an observer.
The Party does not participate in the platform work
and since the rejection by Party Conference of a
resolution asking it so to participate, will not do so.
Representatives on the Confederation are Ian Mikardo
(Chairman International Committee) and Jenny Little
(Head of the International Department).

With the imminence of direct elections it was
decided to intensify the elaboration of a programme to
serve as a common electoral programme for the parties
of the Confederation in the election campaign. Such a
decision was well in line with the tradition of the
1962 Birkelbach Report but went further than the
documents adopted by congresses held in Brussels in
1971 and in Bonn in 1973 (on a social Europe) not
necessarily in terms of how detailed the work would be,
but more in terms of party commitment and dramatic
impact. This was to be a relatively short electoral
document.

The Hague summit of the socialist parties in
November 1974 accepted the principle of such a
programme and a Bureau meeting of November 1975 agreed
on detailed procedures. At the Elsinore meeting of the
Bureau in January 1976 a steering group was set up and
four working parties as follows:

Steering Group (chairman Mr Dröscher - SPD)

Economic Policy (chairman Michel Roccard - PSF)

Social Policy (chairman Mr L. Levi-Sandvi - PSI)
Democracy and Institutions (chairman Mr S. Patijn - PvdA)
External Policy (chairman Mr Bruno Friedrich - SPD)

Each party (two from Italy) excluding the Labour Party has one representative in the Steering Group and one in each sub-group. For some parties one person held several positions. The Danish Social Democrats decided to nominate only their members of the European Parliament.

The groups began work in the Spring of 1976 on the basis of papers which were usually drawn up either by the chairman or by the secretary. Each group held about three meetings and rapidly arrived at consensus about what should be attempted. The proposed programme will take the form of a platform in which emphasis will be placed on a relatively small number of points of salience on which the parties can agree. It has been possible to avoid doctrinal or north/south splits and concentrate less on an ideological basis than on practical proposals, particularly in the economic field - with emphasis on issues such as employment policy. Institutional debate has largely concentrated on the powers of the European Parliament and its relationship with the Commission and the Council. The working groups continued their work until the end of 1976. The 'democratisation' group was the first to terminate its work and the results were considered by the November 1976 meeting of the Bureau in London. The Bureau of the Confederation approved the 37 page platform on 6 June. The completed programme was then to be adopted by the Congress projected in Brussels in Spring 1978.

The platform (adopted without either opposition or approval from Labour Party representatives in the Confederation Bureau) naturally is general in character and at times bears witness to difficult compromises, not least by reference to national solutions for the goal of worker participation and the careful balancing of the continued aim of economic and monetary union with a long series of general economic measures and structural policies as prior conditions. The sections on détente and worker participation raised the greatest problems.

The platform has three main sections: Institutions and Democracy, Economic and Social Policy and External Policy. The section on Institutions proposes that Parliament should acquire a co-legislative power with the Council, but in so doing builds explicitly on present arrangements for a 'concertation' procedure between the two institutions.

The section on Economic and Social Policy is much the longest and most detailed. It proposes to give priority to full employment and as subsidiary goals to the redistribution of wealth (mainly to be handled at the national level) and economic power through such measures as worker participation and control of the activities of large companies. It recognises the need for more coordination of national policies and between national and Community policies, but does not propose any greater degree of supra-nationalisation of economic decision making. It is to some extent surprising that the goal of economic and monetary union is restated – and therefore accepted by the PSF – but it is surrounded by many a qualification and prior condition which will make it a long term goal. At least from a theoretical point of view this aim gives a certain overall coherence to the specific structural and sectorial measures which are proposed.

On External Policy, the platform clearly espouses the view that Europe has an independent role to play in the world, as a balancing factor. It calls for greater conscious acceptance of this fact. Europe must support the maintenance and expansion of détente in concrete directions, through full and detailed application of the Final Act of Helsinki. Europe should play a positive role in increasing the self reliance of the LDCs, in the north/south dialogue, in renewing and expanding the Lomé Convention and in increasing public aid to the LDCs to 0.7 per cent of

GDP.

As a whole the platform would seem to offer the
right degree of generality, with some firm commitments;
the right combination of moderation and originality; to
offer the member parties a loose, but distinctive
framework, which they can each apply in their own
distinctive situation.

The draft platform, whose elaboration had been
dominated by the SPD, did not at first provoke much
reaction, but soon ran into difficulties in several
parties. As was to be expected, there was criticism in
Britain (see Labour Weekly, 5 August 1977) on the
double grounds of its overtly federalist character and
its moderation on matters of economic policy.

Criticism has however spread to those parties which
were involved in the drafting work. The Dutch PvdA has
promised numerous amendments. The Convention of the
French Parti Socialiste held in November 1977 saw
criticism from the CERES minority of the acceptance of
the platform by the Party leadership on the grounds
that it was grist to the mill of the PCF, that the PS
was 'réformiste' or had taken a 'virage a droite'. The
leadership was forced to accept that any acceptance
must remain provisional and that numerous amendments
would have to be tabled. At the Danish Social
Democrats Congress in September, the text of the
platform was distributed and it was praised by the
Prime Minister as a practical example of cooperation
between socialist parties. The document was not on the
agenda and it was for the Party Executive to decide the
Party's position before the Congress of the
Confederation in April. However, references to it from
the floor, as well as comparison with the sections of
the Programme of Principles adopted at the Congress,
dealing with Europe, shows that the institutional
proposals of the Confederation draft are in clear
conflict with social democratic policy.

The SPD Parteitag (Congress) held in Hamburg 15-19
November passed a long resolution on Europe, proposed

by the Executive, which welcomes the platform and with some additions (e.g. consumer policy) would approve it. However, several more critical resolutions were tabled, but were not voted on because of the decision to call a special Parteitag on this issue in February, before the April Congress of the Confederation. Inevitably, this special congress generated amendments to a text which the SPD had hoped would be adopted unchanged.

At the same time, the Confederation has set up a secretariat in Brussels which will eventually have a full time staff of three. The role of the Confederation and its secretariat in a direct elections campaign - both as an organiser of transnational activity and provider of material - is being examined.

Enlargement of the Community to Greece, Spain or Portugal would bring in strong socialist parties from Spain (PSOE, affiliated to the International with 28 per cent of the vote in the Spanish general election) and Portugal, but would probably not increase the relative strength of the socialists in the enlarged Parliament. At the same time, problems of relations with communist parties, the Atlantic alliance and the north/south issue would be sharpened and the dominance of 'Northern' parties in the Confederation reduced. The situation in Greece is rather more confused. (The Panhellenic Party of Mr Papandreou seems opposed to EEC membership.)

The Nationalist or Autonomist Parties have also begun to organise themselves at the European level. A Bureau of Unrepresented Nations (Bretons, Basques, Plaid Cymru, etc.) has existed in Brussels for some time. In March 1977 three such parties went further and created an embryonic organisation, with a basic charter, which was to relate directly to the forthcoming direct elections and which was open to other parties to join. The founder members were the Scottish National Party (SNP), Plaid Cymru and the Belgian Volkunie. The charter emphasises cultural and regional autonomy.

THE RIGHT AND CENTRE RIGHT

a. The Christian Democrats

An early attempt at transnational cooperation among
Christian Democrats was the foundation of the
'Nouvelles Equipes Internationales' (NEI) in 1947.
Here the parties were not represented directly, but
rather national 'teams', which might include a number
of parties and other groups. This led to the formation
in 1961 of the World Union of Christian Democrats
(UMDC) and in 1964 the European Union of Christian
Democrats (UEDC), which together with the South
American body (OCDA) form the regional centres of UMDC.
(30) The sporadic ad hoc conferences of presidents and
secretary generals of the EEC parties which had been
held since 1958 were brought under UEDC and formally
constituted in 1970. This body meets three times a
year and is convoked by the UEDC chairman and the CD
group chairman. This conference tends to devote itself
to thematic discussions rather than specific policy
matters. The group in the European Parliament is also
represented in this body. In April 1972 it was
transformed into the political committee of the CD
parties of the European communities and given a status
as part of the UEDC structure.(31) Until recently the
parties had not evolved a common programme, but
prominent members of national parties frequently
participate in the Journées d'Etudes of the group in
the EP. The most comprehensive statement of principles
by the group or the parties was that contained in the
joint CD group and UEDC report on the political and
constitutional reorganisation of the enlarged Community
(1972); some individual parties have drawn up European
policy programmes, such as the 1972 European policy
action programme of the CDU/CSU.(32)

The Christian Democrats also felt the impact of the
same type of reform movement as we saw in the socialist
camp; here also it was led by a Dutchman, Mr
Westerterp. He launched the idea of a European
People's Party at the June 1970 meeting of the Dutch
branch of UEDC. He sought the establishment of a

European party system and argued that the existing
'interstate' structure of UEDC was inadequate as it
does not lead to binding decisions for the member
parties. The existing parties could affiliate to his
proposed European Christian People's Party, but only if
they accepted a common programme and collective
discipline. In 1972 the parties established a joint
UEDC-EP group working party to examine a common
programme.

The November 1973 congress in Bonn led to an
intensification of the drive towards a European party;
a new chairman, Kai Uwe Von Hassel was elected and
seven working groups were set up, including one on a
common programme and another on European Union.
Further discussion led to enough progress both on party
cooperation and on a manifesto (in train for many
years) to permit the political committee to charge a
group with Mr Lücker and Mr Martens as rapporteurs to
draft a statute for a European party, in September
1975. The statutes and the manifesto were adopted at a
meeting of the political committee in Paris on 21
February 1976.

The formal establishment of the party was delayed
until 29 April 1976(33) in Brussels, due to
differences over its name, which was symbolic of a
deeper divergence over its scope. There were those,
such as the Italian DC and the Belgian PSC/CVP, which
were unwilling to include conservatives and other
'moderates' in the party which would then appear too
right wing and as an anti-socialist bloc which was
unacceptable to parties which must habitually seek
support across the centre, towards the left. The Dutch
Christian Historical Union (in opposition) was unready
to dilute the Christian commitment with non-
confessional conservatism. On the other hand, the
German CDU, and in particular its secretary general
Kurt Biedenkopf, seeks a broad, conservative, non-
confessional, anti-socialist alliance which can
confront the socialists in direct elections.

The broad front view prevailed as to the name

'European People's Party' - Federation of Christian
Democratic Parties of the European Community - in short
a compromise. Different views on the nature of the
party were still evident in the speeches made at the
foundation meeting in Luxemburg on 8 July 1976. For
example Mr Nothomb (PSC) said: 'To create a People's
Party is to create a political force which seeks to
regroup people from all social classes, not merely to
bring them in, but to do so to work for a common ideal
based on solidarity.'

Mr Biedenkopf, on the other hand, placed less
emphasis on the 'social' vocation of the EPP (and hence
eventual to the left or at the least Christian
Democratic Party) and more on its openness to the
centre right: 'The EPP is the basis of a free Europe,
but it is not a closed shop....' However, to date it
is composed solely of Christian Democratic Parties. Mr
Leo Tindemans was elected its president; its vice
presidents are Mr Colin (France), Mr Antoniozzi (Italy)
and Mr Schmelzer (Netherlands). Its political basis is
the European Christian Democratic Manifesto, adopted in
Paris on 21 February 1976. Work is proceeding on the
drawing up of a common electoral programme for the EPP.
The party is well advanced in preparing an electoral
programme which will be based on the European Christian
Democratic Manifesto adopted by UEDC in Paris in
February 1976. A first draft, based on the work of
seven working parties, has been compiled and was
examined by the Political Bureau in its meeting on 25
November 1976. Further amendment and condensation was
then needed to enable a presentation to be prepared for
the 1977 congress.

The statute of the party is strongly federal. The
parties' representation is weighted according to
strength in the European Parliament and its organs can
by majority adopt binding decisions. The role of the
president and the Political Bureau (the political
leadership is exercised by the Bureau) is very wide.
The Bureau is responsible for organising the campaign
for direct elections and proposes changes in the
statute and a draft election platform to the congress.

The policies of the EPP are based on traditional christian democratic concern for the individual and could be summarised in the slogan 'Freedom and Solidarity', but it seeks to remain open to broader centre right cooperations.

b. The Liberals

Cooperation between liberal parties has always been relatively loose and informal. The Liberal International was founded in 1947 at Oxford. Its membership is largely concentrated in the White Commonwealth and in Western Europe (about twenty-five parties). Liberal parties from the Council of Europe also belong to the Liberal Movement for a United Europe.(34) The basic statements of liberal principles are the two Oxford declarations of 1947 and 1967. These are both, of course, very general, but in them can be discerned the fundamental liberal concern with political and economic freedom adapted to modern conditions. By 1967 there was a greater recognition of the need for some state intervention in economic and social life, but limited to the strict minimum.

The 1972 congress of the Liberal International adopted a resolution asking the party leaders to examine the practicality of setting up a Federation of Liberal Parties in the European communities. The reaction was positive and a working party, in which Mr Talsma and Mr De Koster, both Dutchmen, were very active, was set up and reported to the 1974 Florence congress. The congress adopted a draft statute which was left to the individual parties to ratify.(35)

The founding congress was held in Stuttgart on 26-27 March 1976, elected Gaston Thorn President of the Federation, and adopted the Stuttgart declaration. The German FDP, Dutch PVV, Belgian PLP/PVV/PL, Danish Venstre and the French Parti Radical et Radical Socialiste Républicain joined at that time. Subsequently, the Italian Liberal Party (PLI) and the Italian Republican Party (PRI) joined as did the French radicaux de gauche.(36) The Liberal Assembly held in

Llandudno in September 1976 finally ratified British membership. The Danish Radikale Venstre joined. The French Republicains independants (Giscardians) joined at the November 1976 congress. The arrival of the Giscardians caused the British delegation to table a critical motion in the congress which was, however, not voted upon. Mr Thorn simply insisted on the right of the Giscardians as founder participants to ratify membership. Few imagine that the British Liberal Party will now reconsider its membership. The same cannot be said of the Mouvement des Radicaux de Gauche who responded by 'suspending' their participation and declaring that they would reconsider their position. Their withdrawal appears likely (but is not certain), since, as cosignatories of the 'Programme Commun' with the PS and PCF, their relations with the RI would be delicate and their position as partners with the Union of the Left possibly compromised.

The party held its first congress in The Hague on 6 and 7 November 1976 where the work of the seven original working parties (human rights, European institutions, agriculture, economics and finance, regional policy, foreign policy, defence, investment and standard of living) was examined.(37) Three new working parties were added: self employed and small and medium sized businesses, social policy, energy. There was wide agreement on the main outline of a common programme, but some issues such as the powers of the elected European Parliament, regional policy, foreign policy - in particular relations with the United States - and defence required further study. The working groups were able to present reports in early 1977 which were consolidated into a programme by May 1977 for adoption at the 1977 congress. Mr Thorn was confirmed as president and Mr Genscher and Mr De Koster were elected vice presidents. The British Bureau members are: David Steel, Russell Johnston, Mrs Holmstead and the Party's international liaison officer.

As for the Christian Democrats, there are problems about the range of views which should be permitted in the Federation. The three declarations give only the broadest indication of what kind of liberalism is espoused by the Federation. There are at least two types found in the Community: classic liberalism and 'social' liberalism; some liberals emphasise their lay political origin, others do not. Some have traditionally taken part in centre left coalitions (Danish Radikale Venstre, FDP since 1969) and others in centre right coalitions (Belgian, Dutch and Italian parties). The key issue was the admission of the Giscardians (who only decided to join at the November 1976 congress) although their members sit in the Liberal Group in the European Parliament and the Italian PRI. The British Liberals were extremely reticent about the admission of both these parties. At the 1975 Liberal Assembly an amendment was carried seeking to define more closely the political objectives of the Federation and opposing 'conservative parties and in particular the Fédération Nationale des Républicains Indépendants'.(38) The recent changes in the PLI and the absence so far of the Giscardians has made it possible for the party to join.(39) The parties in the Federation do indeed cover a very wide range of views from the Radicaux de Gauche who are cosignatories of the Programme Commun with the socialists and communists to the Benelux and Italian liberals, passing through the Danish social liberals and the British party.

The main originality of the statute is its extremely federal character. Binding decisions can be made by a two-thirds majority in the congress on both matters relating to the European communities as such and to European union. The liberals have perhaps of all the party groupings the least reticence about supranationality both in the Community institutions and in party arrangements. Article 10 makes it clear that the liberal group (and future directly elected group) has an organic link with the Federation, as 'its' group. Membership of the congress is based on a mixed formula of a basic representation of six members per country (shared if necessary as between parties) and additional members based on votes obtained in national elections, which will ensure the British Liberal Party the largest delegation.

Enlargement of the Community to Spain, Greece or Portugal would not bring any major increase in strength to the group, unless the Greek Centre Union were to be considered a liberal party. Equally, the Portugese Popular Democrats (PPD) might also join.

c. The other parties of the centre right

The 1975 Conservative Party Conference voted in favour of a 'moderate centre right alliance (a European Democrat Party)'. It is clear that the Conservatives see the danger of entering direct elections isolated without continental allies. The party has participated in a loose grouping, the European Union of Conservatives which goes beyond the Community and covers the CDU and RPR as well as the Scandinavian conservative parties. Sir Christopher Soames has been active in promoting the concept of a broad alliance, anti-socialist in character. He saw the best future for the Conservative Party in Europe in '............ participation in an effective organisation of the centre, joining us with the traditions of other parties and other nations'.(40) The basis of this alliance would be, in terms of political philosophy, support for the social market economy and freedom of the individual.

The Gaullist RPR is currently the main component of the European Progressive Democrats (with Fianna Fail and the Danish Progress Party). These parties have no obvious place in any European grouping and the EDP group may not seem any more than a marriage of circumstance. This may not be entirely true in that there is a common basis in support for the common agricultural policy, an institutional pragmatism and the fact that at least Fianna Fail and RPR are parties similar in origin - mass national movements based on political action, one historic figure who became synonymous with their nations - de Gaulle and de Valera.(41) Such considerations might keep the EDP group together, but it would not organise a European

118

party for the elections. If RPR strength falls in 1978 these three parties might be available to join a conservative alliance or a wider centre right grouping. Against this must be mentioned the strong anti-European current which has revived in the RPR under Jacques Chirac.

A CENTRE RIGHT ALLIANCE

As we have seen, a wider European union of conservatives does exist, bridging many elements of the centre right since it has included conservatives, the CDU and UDR. However, it has not included all christian democratic nor indeed any liberal parties. CDU Secretary General Biedenkopf has argued in favour of creating an 'outer circle'(42) - the European Democratic Union which would unite in a loose grouping all the elements of the centre right: Christian Democrats, Conservatives, Liberals, Gaullists and other 'People's Parties'. Such an alliance, which would have little machinery, but which would organise periodic 'summits' of centre right leaders, would act in parallel to closer cooperation between groups in the European Parliament (especially Christian Democrat and Conservative). Ultimately, the goal would be the enlargement of the European People's Party to include other elements.

A meeting was held in Salzburg in September 1975 to discuss the formation of the EDU, which was attended by Mr Whitelaw. Draft statutes have been drawn up and the initial nucleus is intended to be the CDU, British Conservatives and a number of other conservative parties, including some from the smaller European democracies outside the Community. It is intended that the Liberals and other Christian Democrat parties should join in due course.

A number of problems stand in the way of this project - and indeed a meeting of the proto-EDU in Austria was recently postponed. The British Tories have not committed themselves to this precise form of

centre right alliance. The bureaucratic opposition of
existing organisations already a feature of the
landscape - the EPP and the Liberal Federation are
obstacles. At the same time, as we have seen, there
are genuine ideological objections of substance in both
the Liberal and the EPP groupings. There is also some
suspicion of CDU motives, and problems about leadership
and dominance in such a wide centre right grouping.
Some British Conservatives prefer independence, ad hoc
election time alliances and parliamentary cooperation
to a tight centre right alliance. Furthermore, the EDU
has the defect, at the moment, of being almost entirely
Northern European in inspiration and substance. It
could be dangerous for the centre right cause to become
a Northern European cause - political and geographical
cleavages should be cross cutting. At a meeting in
Munich in March 1977 it was decided to proceed with the
EDU. It included christian parties and conservatives
(both the Conservative Party and RPR) from within and
without the EEC. However, the Italian DC and the
Benelux parties (CDA, PSC/CVP, PCS) refused to
participate in the meeting.(42a)

It might be that in the absence of history, of
national alliances, of labels and pre-existing
organisation, a rational centre right alliance could be
formed, perhaps composed of the CDU, British and Danish
Conservatives, Irish Fianna Faíl, Benelux (but not
Luxemburg) Liberal Parties, Italian Liberals and
perhaps the Danish Venstre as well as the Republicains
independants, but not the UDR which at least in terms
of image does not think of itself as a right wing or
conservative party. Such a group might obtain as many
as 115-20 seats out of 410 in a directly elected
parliament, making it by far larger than the other
right of centre groups. However, such historical and
other factors most definitely cannot be discounted.

REPRESENTATION IN THE
ELECTED PARLIAMENT

At this stage it is very hard to predict the likely

outcome of election, as a great deal would depend on decisions about electoral systems, party alliance, turnout and the general 'conjoncture politique' in which the elections take place. Some tentative projections have been made for the United Kingdom, Holland and Ireland.(43) Even these projections must be accepted only with the greatest caution having regard to the large number of variable factors, such as those enumerated above.

A careful examination of the situation gives a likely distribution or range of distribution of the kind indicated in Table 2 in the Appendix.(44) A certain number of interesting conclusions emerge from the Table. The outcome for the main blocs would be:

Socialists	111 - 142
Communists	47 - 56
Combined Left	158 - 198
Christian Democrats	83 - 93
Conservatives	36 - 51
Centre Right	119 - 144
Liberals	35 - 38
EPD	28 - 36
Others	18 - 20

These figures are based on the assumption that existing electoral systems are used with little modification and presuppose party conflict roughly along existing lines. The socialists are seen as being the most affected by political conditions, with relatively large changes in their position being possible.

As is clear, no firm majority can be expected to emerge. The socialist group should become the largest single group. Even in the best circumstances (e.g.

SPD, Labour and French PS 'highs') the combined left would be just tantalisingly short of an overall majority in the Assembly.

The Christian Democrats alone cannot expect to recover the position of dominance which they enjoyed in the 1950s and early 1960s. Even the promised broad centre right bloc of conservatives and christian democrats could not expect to gain control and might not even obtain more seats than the socialists alone.

The broadest centre right including Liberals and Christian Democrats and Conservatives could not form an absolute majority and might barely obtain more seats than the socialists.

The European progressive democrats may not survive as a group especially since the Gaullist RDR could in certain circumstances obtain far fewer seats than postulated here (to the benefit of the Socialist and Liberal Groups). Only with the union of all the forces of the centre right including the EPD could that alliance be sure to control the Assembly and even then might have to rely on support from 'others', a group of heterogeneous political character which the disintegration of the EPD might inflate. Such a 'union of the right' would be extremely difficult to engineer.

At this stage it is, of course, difficult to suggest any firm conclusion as to the type of political strategies that these parameters will impose. At the same time, a number of points do emerge from an analysis of likely voting patterns and from the high and low tide positions for blocs of parties.

The first point is that direct elections under the proposed scheme will cause little major shift in the present balance of power in the Assembly. It would be likely that the combined left would be slightly strengthened and the centre right and liberal bloc slightly weakened, but not conclusively.

The role of the European Parliament will not be to

122

form and sustain an executive; its role will correspond
more to that played by the United States Congress, or
by the Swiss Parliament which is faced with an all
party executive which it can in theory dismiss, but
which is in practice permanent and even unaffected by
election results. No firm majority is needed in such a
body. However, it is vitally important for the future
image and effectiveness of the EP that it should choose
a coherent policy direction. This requires the
formation of a cohesive majority which can unite round
certain clear and well defined policy options.

In the formation of such a 'management bloc' which
will be able, if it is tightly organised, to control
the Presidency, the Bureau, the Committee
chairmanships, nomination of rapporteurs, the agenda
and procedural issues, the left will be pivotal. With
only small additional support the left, if united,
could organise the Assembly and give coherent
leadership. The left will need to emphasise those
aspects of its policies which 1. will unite the left,
2. act as bridge builders to progressives who do not
desire total right-left polarisation, which would force
a difficult choice upon them. This must represent less
an abandonment of principles for a compromise than a
choice of priorities in the interest of a strategic
design.

Priority should be given to those issues which can
command widespread support among christian social and
other progressive non-socialist forces. The aim should
be to promote broad cooperation and block the formation
of a polarised, anti-socialist centre right grouping,
which could command a majority in Parliament.

The most responsive parties to such an approach will
be those who, at the national level reject most firmly
a rigid right-left polarisation of political life.
These are some Benelux christian parties, the French
radicals, Danish centre parties and some small Dutch
parties.

These groups share with the socialists a concern for

a humane democratic and decentralised Community. They do not reject, a priori, greater state intervention in economic life, especially where necessary to cushion the effects of rapid change, to protect declining sectors of the economic and disadvantaged regions or population groups (e.g. rural areas). There could be common ground in support for a more progressive and generous social policy, with an interventionist social fund; for workers' participation; for an active regional policy with a larger fund; for structural reform in agriculture and for a more generous trade policy with respect to developing countries.

Discussions among the groups concerned would reveal what common ground did exist and what could be achieved without abandoning fundamental positions. Emphasis on issues linking these groups together, rather than divisive issues, would tend to prevent the emergence of a strong centre right bloc.

In regard to European institutional reform, a broader alliance, encompassing christian democrats and Italian communists could be reached. Its leitmotiv would be a more vigorous assertion of the existing powers of the Parliament to achieve concrete, substantive and symbolic political change, as a prelude to stepping up pressure for more powers. Pressure for more powers should appear only as a logical and necessary culmination of the activity of the Parliament.

No clear strategy towards the communists is envisaged at this point. The major communist parties in the Community are in interesting stages of development, whose outcome is hard to predict. Furthermore, the Italian and the French parties retain considerable divergences on European policy. Much will depend on future developments. Without any alliance, communists and socialists will vote together on many issues. On some matters, agreement might be possible with the Italian party.

As we have seen, the European parties will not in the first instance represent a major force and will not enjoy any large degree of autonomy from the member parties. Many obstacles will continue to stand in the way of their development, but their mere existence has considerable symbolic importance which should not be underestimated. In any event the future depends to a considerable extent on the political parties, European and national.

ACCOUNTABILITY

It is an axiom of representative democracy that elected representatives should be held accountable to their electors. In national politics, where ready made constitutional and party machinery has long existed, there are frequent complaints that accountability is illusory. In the novel European setting, where machinery must be invented from zero, this will, not least because of the inevitable size of the constituencies, be a special problem once members of the European Parliament are directly elected.

Up to now, MEPs have, by virtue of the dual mandate, always been members of their national parliaments and have, therefore, been accountable to their parties and electorates in the normal way. Apart from the fact that the European Parliament seats are 'party seats' which means that MEPs depend on their home parties for nomination, no special accountability procedures exist. In some parties, MEPs give periodic reports on their European activity. This has particularly been the case of the German SPD and CDU. Each party sends an official of the Fraktion to party sessions, a paper is circulated in the Fraktion on the results of sessions and there is a Committee of the Fraktion on European Affairs. In other parties accountability has been less formal and more sporadic. European work will only be a very limited element in the accountability of an MEP to his constituents because he will be judged almost exclusively on his national party's image. Even if Europe as such were an issue in an election, it would affect MEPs and others equally.

With direct elections the situation must change. First, there will be more European MPs (in Britain up to forty for each major party) and after a transitional period the double mandate will disappear, or be confined to a few exceptional cases. Each MEP, with constituencies of over 500,000 in the large member states, will be accountable, as is a national MP, directly to his electors. In those states such as Britain, France and Ireland, where close constituency relations have been traditional, the question of accountability arises all the more acutely.

A member in Britain will be selected as a candidate by some ad hoc European constituency party organisation selection conference. Parties will have to examine how, outside election periods contact can be maintained and accountability to the party ensured. Traditional methods of 'nursing a constituency' will be impossible; MEPs will no longer be able to maintain an 'artisanal' approach to constituency relations. The problem will have a US dimension and indeed much can be learned from the manner in which US legislators can maintain relations with constituencies of well over 500;000 voters. People who argue that MEPs in such large seats would become unaccountable would be surprised to discover that American legislators are far more directly accountable to their district than British MPs are, and that public sentiment on an issue can much more easily work its way through and influence an American legislator who cannot ignore such expressions of opinion.

MEPs will have to be given the resources needed to carry out such a task. They will need a personal staff, as distinct from group secretariats. Their staff will be partly at the seat of the Parliament and partly in their constituency. With the MEP in Brussels/Strasbourg or Luxemburg, it will be the duty of one or two staff members working in his constituency to monitor developments there and to make the first contacts with individuals and organisations which can then be followed up by the member himself. At the same time creative use should be made of local and regional

news media - local press, television and radio. Local
stations might stage debates on the impact of Europe on
the region between MEPs of opposed parties. Much will
depend on the way in which the work of the EP develops,
especially as to what extent individual case work or
local representational functions will fall to MEPs. It
may well be that in many areas, MEPs' main contacts
will be with well established European and national
lobbies on global issues. It should, however, not be
overlooked that in regions with declining industries,
serious unemployment problems and large rural
populations Community intervention instruments - Coal
and Steel Community Funds, the Social and Regional
Funds, Transport infrastructure pricing, the European
Investment Bank, policies on state aids and external
protectionism (steel and textiles) can have a major
impact on employment and living standards. It follows
that in such areas - South Wales and the Liège-
Charleroi area of Belgium being prime examples - the
role of MEPs may be nearly as closely related to
micro-level problems as at national level.

At the national level too the problem of
accountability arises. Some would argue that this is
not a problem in that, having ensured the direct
accountability and democratic legitimacy of MEPs who
will sit in a European Parliament, it would be wrong to
imply any subordinate relationship with any national
institutions. Such a view is a purist one which does
not take account of real susceptibilities, at least in
some new member states. Without imposing a subordinate
status on MEPs, it would seem imperative to link them
into the national political scene, if only on a
liaison basis. Otherwise they will float in a loose
and disembodied way. Since no direct accountability
can exist to European parties - though European group
discipline and accountability is an issue which must be
looked at - it is reasonable that national parties
should have a droit de regard on what their MEPs are
doing.

This could be achieved through several devices: in
Britain the senior MEP could sit in the shadow cabinet

if the party was in opposition or in the 1922-Committee Executive or the liaison committee when parties were in government. MEPs could have non-voting status in party meetings and Parliamentary Party Committees. They could have the same rights as national MPs and candidates to participate in organs of the mass party outside Parliament and in party conferences.

As to relations with the national parliament itself, a variety of ideas has been put forward in various countries which reflect the nuances of attitude which exist on this problem. Some desire a system as close as practical to the dual mandate which would tend to bind MEPs closely into the domestic political structure; others desire only to ensure a two way flow of information. In Germany, the 'Berlin solution' offers an immediate precedent. The Berlin members of the Bundestag are non-voting members, who otherwise have full rights of membership. It is likely that this solution will be adopted in Germany for all or some of the MEPs. In Holland, it has been suggested by Mr Patijn that the Dutch MEPs should be 'special' members of the Dutch Parliament (which chamber is unspecified); such a view has been supported by Foreign Minister van der Stoel,(45) but has been contested by the opposition Liberal Party.

In Britain and other member states with a weaker or non-elected chamber some proposals have centred on ex-officio membership of those Houses. In Britain these have centred on temporary membership of the House of Lords,(46) though Mr Michael Stewart has proposed non-voting membership of the House of Commons. Eight organisations giving evidence to the House of Commons Select Committee suggested this solution. The House of Lords Select Committee was less than satisfied with the concept; however, it did not oppose it. In the Lords debate on 29 March 1976, the government gave no indication of its thinking on the matter. Neither report of the Commons Select Committee expresses a view.

Other proposals have been put forward. At the

128

previously mentioned ELEC Conference in May 1976, there
was considerable discussion on the issue. Mr Heath
suggested non-voting membership of the Commons for
MEPs. Lord Gladwyn approved of the 'Berlin status'
idea. Mr Stewart (Lab. Fulham) and Mr Hurd (Con. mid-
Oxon) considered this proposal probably unacceptable to
the Commons and preferred a Grand Committee to which
MEPs would belong.(47) Such a committee, with
appropriate sub-committees could undertake continuous
scrutiny of European affairs and enable an adequate
exchange of information. It would not, of course, keep
MEPs involved in domestic politics and issues, which is
of course important. This might more naturally occur
through parallel participation in the parliamentary
parties and party committees.

In Britain the problem of regional representation
will arise. Scottish and Welsh members (and not only
Nationalists) will regard themselves as regional
representatives, as will the Ulster members. Some
English members will equally represent clearly
identifiable regions (Cornwall). In Scotland and
Wales the Labour Party at least will allow the regional
party considerable autonomy in the choice of candidates
and manifesto for the elections to the devolved
Assemblies. Inevitably, the question will arise of
regional 'accountability'. Scottish and Welsh MEPs
will have to be given status in relation to their
regional party organisation and in relation to the
Assembly. The Commons Select Committee recommends that
the dual mandate Assembly - European Parliament be
permitted. This might be physically less difficult
than the dual mandate Westminster - European
Parliament. The Assemblies could make arrangements
through their committee structures to liaise with their
regional MEPs. The SNP proposed in evidence to the
Commons Select Committee that MEPs in Scotland should
have non-voting membership of the Scottish Assembly.
(48)

The Lords Select Committee concluded that there was
no immediate ideal solution to these problems. Lords'
membership, devolved Assembly-European Parliament dual

mandate, Grand Committees and participation in the existing scrutiny committees all offered some advantages. In the view of the Select Committee the whole matter should be reviewed by the committee now set up to 'consider the practice and procedure of Parliament'.(49) Certainly this is a problem which must be solved.

Whatever the development of European parties in the future and whatever machinery may be designed by national parties and parliaments to ensure mutual information and accountability, it is clear that a network of new and at times complicated political relationships will have been created. These relationships, obligations and constraints will have to be dovetailed into the work of the political groups in the European Parliament. The obligations of members will have to be balanced; party discipline and policy making arrangements at the European level will have to take these constraints into account. This would lead no doubt to the laxer party discipline and looser political coalitions characteristic of Federal Legislatures such as the United States Congress. As long as the nomination process and major policy making procedures continue to be controlled by the lower national level (as is of course the case in the US), the sanctions available to the European parliamentary groups and party organisations will be strictly limited. These sanctions may prove inadequate in that a member might find that the consequences of defying national party agencies were considerably more serious. In view of the fragility of European party organisation, direct confrontation with national party agencies might in the first phase be highly undesirable. The European parties may therefore be expected to affirm their existence and expand their role only slowly and prudently.

NOTES

(1) 'Parlamento Europeo: Un rosso molto annacquato' in Il Mondo, 25 August 1976.

(2)   See remarks by Mr Dangerfeld, Sir George
Middleton, Mr Heath and Lord Gladwyn on this issue at
the European League for Economic Cooperation (ELEC)
Conference on direct elections, held in May 1976.
Report pp.35-7. Mr Heath recognised that there could
be a greater role for independents and representatives
of non-party organisations than in national elections.
(2a) See Terkel Nielsen, 'European Groups and the
decision making process: the Common Agricultural
Policy', in The New Politics of European Integration,
Macmillan, 1972.
(2b) ETUC statement on direct elections.
(3)   Douglas Hurd, Conservative spokesman on Europe,
expressed this view at the ELEC Conference. Report
pp.51-2.
(4)   The Times, 6 September 1976, p.2.
(5)   Report of the National Executive Committee (1976)
p.9.
(6)   Douglas Hurd, at the ELEC Conference, report p.53.
(7)   See debate in the European Parliament on oral
questions H 128/76 from Mr Schuijt Debates 13 October
1976. A distinction was made between the proposal for
the Commission to organise a campaign on support for
parties.
(8)   Douglas Hurd, ELEC Conference, report p.67.
(9)   H. Vredeling in The Common Market of Political
Parties, reprinted in The New Politics of European
Integration, ed. G. Ionesco, Macmillan, 1972, pp.98-137.
(10) For useful accounts of the history and position of
European parties see: European Political Parties, ed.
S. Henig and J. Pinder, Praeger 1970; Social Democracy
in post war Europe, W. Paterson and I. Campbell,
Macmillan 1974; The Communist Parties of Western
Europe, N. McInnes, OUP 1975.
(11) Feld, W.J., Non-governmental forces and world
politics, Praeger 1972, p.214f.
(12) Henig and Pinder, eds. op.cit.
(13) Anderson, S.V., The Nordic Council, University of
Washington Press 1967, pp.63-9 and pp.98-9.
(14) eg Anderson op.cit.
(15) For the activity of these groups see Fitzmaurice,
J., The Party Groups in the European Parliament, D.C.
Heath 1975, especially chs.3-9 and chapter 11.

(16) See Vredeling, H. op.cit.

(17) For an analysis of these issues see Vredeling, H. op.cit. and G. Bonvincini, Interaction between parliamentary institutions and political forces, in European Integration and the future of Parliaments in Europe, European Parliament 1975, pp.174-8 and Guizzi Vincento, Una tentativa di rinovamento della sinistra in Europe in Socialismo '70, June-July 1970.

(18) See Feld, W., op.cit., pp.221-3, McInnes, op.cit. pp.160-207, Fitzmaurice, op.cit. pp.129-42.

(19) Pravda, 26 August 1962, p.3.

(20) Timmermann, H., I Communisti dell'Europa occidentale et la CEE.

(21) Quoted in Timmermann, H., op.cit.

(22) Amendola quoted in UNITA, 26 January 1974, p.1.

(23) Timmermann op.cit.

(24) Georges Marchais, Le Monde, 27 January 1974.

(25) McInnes, N., op.cit.

(26) Feld, W.J., op.cit.

(27) Bonvincini op.cit., pp.174-7.

(28) Vredeling op.cit. pp.129-30 and Speranza, G., Partito progressista, Partito Socialista Europea in December 1969, p.793.

(29) Rules of procedure document PE/GE/26/74 and press release PS/CE/25/74.

(30) Feld, W., op.cit., pp.219-20.

(31) Der Traum von Europa, R. Lewandowski, Rheinischer Merkur 15 June 1973 and Müller, J., Bedeutung und Notwendigkeit der Integration der Politischen Parteien auf der Europäisches Ebene und Ihre Zusammenwirkung, pp.4-8.

(32) Fitzmaurice op.cit. chapter 4.

(33) Agence Europe, 30 April 1976.

(34) Feld, W., p.220.

(35) See VVD (Dutch Liberal Party) Journal for VVD Congress 1975. Statement by Mr Robert Fabre at the colloquium on foreign policy on 26 September 1976.

(36) Quoted in Le Quotidien de Paris, 27 September 1976 p.3.

(37) European Report, 9 November 1976, p.3.

(38) Motion moved by Russell Johnston and amendment by Gordon Lishman.

(39) See reports from the Liberal Assembly 1976: The

Guardian, 17 September 1976, p.11.

(40) See Financial Times, 20 September 1976, p.11.

(41) See speech by Mr Lynch to the EDP study days in County Clare quoted in The Irish Press, 8 September 1976, p.3: 'We here equate Mr de Valera and General de Gaulle.'

(42) Interview in Europa Union, March 1976.

(42a) Neue Zuricher Zeitung, 17 March 1977.

(43) For British see Table 1. For Ireland see article in the Irish Times, Direct to Europe, 20 September 1976 p.10.

(44) Source: The Economist, 30 September 1976, p.61.

(45) Het Financiële Dagblad, 13 September 1976, p.8.

(46) See evidence of various organisations to the Select Committee of the House of Commons on Direct Elections to the European Assembly – First Report pp. 12-7.

(47) ELEC Conference Report pp.65-6.

(48) House of Commons SC, First Report pp.12-7.

(49) House of Lords SC on the European Communities, 22nd Report, paras. 31-7, and House of Commons SC, Third Report, paras. 37-42. The SC was cautious about formal links, but did recognise the need for at the very least some informal or party links.

APPENDIX
TABLE 1

Votes cast for the main parties (as per cent of all
votes cast) in October 1974, in 78 possible European
parliamentary constituencies in Britain.

Totals may not add up to 100 per cent because of votes
for minor parties (see footnote).

	Con.	Lab.	Lib.	Nat.
Croydon	47.1	29.0	23.3	–
SW London	45.1	30.2	24.2	–
Harrow	42.8	39.2	16.5	–
West London	44.2	41.2	13.7	–
Enfield	39.2	39.7	17.1	–
Heathrow	38.7	44.4	15.3	–
Ilford	36.1	45.9	17.0	–
SE London	34.2	48.8	15.8	–
Wandsworth	32.7	52.4	13.9	–
East London	23.7	57.3	14.2	–
Central London	23.1	61.2	12.9	–
Dorset	49.9	23.0	26.9	–
Weald	50.4	23.4	25.7	–
Portsmouth	50.5	24.2	25.0	–
Sussex	51.3	24.7	24.0	–
Devon	45.2	22.3	32.3	–
Surrey	48.9	24.8	25.4	–
Cornwall	44.0	25.4	29.8	–
Somerset	43.4	28.1	27.9	–
Fens	44.9	29.5	25.6	–
Upper Thames	46.2	31.6	21.2	–
East Kent	45.3	31.3	22.9	–
Solent	42.4	29.8	27.2	–
Suffolk	45.7	33.3	20.7	–
Gloucs & Wilts	42.5	31.0	26.4	–
Berkshire	42.0	31.2	26.0	–
North Essex	42.2	34.7	23.1	–
Chilterns	42.8	35.6	21.5	–
West Kent	42.6	35.5	20.7	–
South Essex	39.7	35.6	24.5	–

	Con.	Lab.	Lib.	Nat.
Norfolk	43.2	38.9	17.8	–
Herts	40.7	37.6	21.1	–
Northampton	41.3	40.0	18.7	–
Avon	37.6	41.6	20.1	–
SW Midlands	43.9	28.7	27.4	–
Leicester	41.3	38.8	17.5	–
South Birmingham	39.8	42.5	17.1	–
Derby	38.1	44.5	17.1	–
Nottingham	37.8	44.8	16.5	–
North Birmingham	37.1	45.9	16.1	–
Coventry	36.0	45.5	18.0	–
Dudley	37.0	46.9	15.8	–
Stoke-on-Trent	36.1	48.0	16.0	–
Wolverhampton	31.8	50.9	14.2	–
NE Midlands*	30.8	50.8	14.8	–
East Cheshire	44.7	28.8	26.5	–
North Yorkshire	44.6	30.9	23.7	–
West Lancashire	45.1	35.6	19.3	–
Cumbria	43.8	37.4	18.7	–
East Yorkshire	40.5	35.0	24.3	–
West Cheshire	41.6	40.4	17.8	–
NE Lancashire	38.5	44.1	16.4	–
Bradford	34.0	46.0	19.6	–
Bolton	34.4	48.5	16.5	–
South Humberside	32.5	46.4	21.0	–
Rochdale	31.3	47.1	20.9	–
Northumberland*	29.5	46.5	18.4	–
Cleveland	31.8	53.8	14.2	–
Manchester	30.9	53.8	14.8	–
Liverpool	31.5	55.9	12.2	–
Durham	28.6	54.2	17.2	–
Leeds	27.9	53.2	18.5	–
Warrington	28.0	57.0	14.9	–
Tyne & Wear	26.4	57.1	16.4	–
Sheffield*	24.6	57.6	14.7	–
SW Yorks	21.5	57.6	20.4	–
North Wales	29.2	36.0	21.0	13.8
Cardiff	25.6	52.7	13.9	7.2
SE Wales	21.9	57.6	12.4	7.9

	Con.	Lab.	Lib.	Nat.
SW Wales	19.4	51.2	15.1	14.1
Highlands	31.5	14.9	15.1	38.4
NE Scotland	28.3	27.5	9.7	34.4
SW Scotland	29.8	33.2	10.8	26.2
Lothian	29.9	36.1	9.4	24.5
South Clydeside	24.4	41.8	8.0	25.6
Upper Clyde	19.8	44.1	5.4	30.5
Central Scotland	17.3	40.2	4.8	37.4
North Clydeside	17.8	47.9	4.6	28.5

*In these three areas a significant Labour rebel vote
in October 1974 affects the totals; otherwise any
significant other vote is for the National Front.

APPENDIX
TABLE 2

	Socia-lists	Christian Democrats	Lib.	European Progressive Democrats	Con.	Comm. & Allies	Others	Total Seats
Belgium	7	7	3			1	4-6	24
Denmark	4- 6	(1)	2-3	2- 4	1	1	(1)	16
France	32-30	2	15	20-25		16-20		81
Germany	32-40	34-42	7					81
Ireland	3	6		6				15
Italy	8-13	28	1-3			26-31	6	81
Luxemburg	2	2	1			1		6
Netherlands	6- 9	6-10	5-8			1	1	25
United Kingdom(1)	27-46				35-50		6	81

(1) Assumes 'first past the post' system is used.
    Were PR to be used the Liberals could obtain 6-10 seats.

5 The European Parliament in transition

The Community is undoubtedly at a crossroads. Direct elections may in the medium or long term create a dynamic which will lead to a more politicised Community with more powers and a wider role, with greater popular control and greater popular impact. On the other hand, if direct elections fail to create this dynamic, then there is no other conceivable basis on which the Community can achieve a breakthrough to a more politicised role. Then the Community might remain a customs union with certain associated common policies. This does not, of course, mean that such a situation is not viable; indeed, it might be both considered viable and desirable for some of those political forces which opposed the Community. It must be said though, that in the long term such a limited outcome cannot offer any positive perspective.

These then are the alternatives: a gradual widening and deepening of the political role of the Community or stagnation. This choice should not be presented as a choice between federation or collapse, because a whole range of outcomes - stopping well short of federation, but giving the Community a political dimension can be imagined. Events and the political will of the citizens of the Community will determine how far the Community will reach in this range of options. The degree of centralised power; the relationship between the Community institutions, and between the Community and member states will all be determined by these factors. No outcome is predetermined; indeed, direct elections themselves offer no guaranteed outcome; offer no guarantee of political progress. They offer an opportunity which must be seized by politicians and the electorate. Nor is it self evident that the directly elected Parliament

will necessarily promote integration as it has been
perceived up to now.

It is clear that centrifugal tendencies will emerge
in the Parliament. The political debate will centre as
much around the pace and direction of the development
of the Community as around classic right-left issues
although these will retain considerable motive force.
At the same time it is evident that the very existence
of an elected Parliament will lead to a deepening and
widening of the political dimension of the Community
and will give Community politics a new character. The
Community will move from predominantly bureaucratic
politics to politics pure and simple. Whatever
happens, this will be a significant change which should
in time do much to alter the character of the Community.

The future of the European Parliament and indeed the
dynamic of direct elections cannot be considered in
isolation from the global development of the Community.
Before we can look at the probable scenarios for the
development of the European Parliament itself, we must
fix the framework in which it will move. We must be
clear about the limits which will be imposed on the
Community's development.

Many of the early theories of integration appear to
have read too much into the early rapid progress which
the Community made in the period 1958-65.(1) They were
led to predict that the increasing degree of economic
integration would rapidly enmesh more and more sectors
of the economy until the customs union had become an
economic union, and the economic union a political
union. Such a development would be irreversible and
would of itself create linkage between economic and
political integration, as it became increasingly
impossible to maintain the existing level of economic
integration and the integrity of common policies
without moving towards closer political integration
expressed through common political institutions and
decision making. Many even saw the distinction between
'high politics' and 'low politics' breaking down. The
creation of a political Community would then become

automatic and irreversible, leading to cooperation in the sensitive areas of foreign policy, defence and macro-economic management.

This has not happened. Such theories seemed to describe accurately the first phase of the development of the Community, when the resistance of integration seemed to disappear with what seems in retrospect a strange and disconcerting ease. From here to generalisations about future development there was a dangerous gap. Resistance to integration first developed in some different sectors and in different time periods. There was a gradual stiffening. The immediate post war period, with its special atmosphere and convergence of events, was over and the reflexes expressed by General de Gaulle were certainly also felt in other countries; especially in new member states after 1973.

The essential ambiguity of the Community has not been resolved: how, with intergovernmental machinery, do you create a supra-national Community which depends for its legitimacy on the willingness of national governments to pool sovereignty in the Community institutions? Of course no other way exists. This is precisely the creative tension which has brought some of the greatest steps forward. However, this method has very real limits. It may be that these limits are moveable, but only gradually, and without confrontation with the stronger centres of national resistance to integration.

Such theoretical analysis and even more so the practice of the Community has always been ambivalent as to the exact limits of this 'integration logic'.(2) It was always less than totally clear what stimuli of an external character would be required from time to time to keep the process going and to overcome blockage. There is too ambivalence as to the nature of such stimuli, if required. Would they represent quantative changes in the nature of the integration process or merely periodic impulsions in order to rectify slackening momentum?

Some early theories seemed to postulate (as we have shown) an automatic self-perpetuating process and never explained what finite limits, as to both goals, means and resistance might be encountered.

The governments and indeed the 'intergovernmentalist' school of thought recognised and indeed insisted that the Community was a creation of the existing nation states and had not escaped from their control. For governments, the process had created interdependence which might raise the cost of independent action contrary to the Community spirit, but which by no means made it impossible. The condition of automaticity and irreversibility are from being accepted by governments. For them any new impetus must come from their express political will. Indeed all 'official' attempts to create a political union (for example the Fouchet Plan or the Economic and Monetary Union approach) up to and including the Tindemans Report have been based on this premise. Here a political Community could not come about in opposition to the states nor would it supplant them. It would be their creation and would obtain its legitimacy from the consent and support of governments. Such a process would be controlled and limited. Of course, the hard core Gaullists and British and Danish anti-marketeers paradoxically fear that the early theorists could be right and that such a process would acquire an automatic momentum unless it were deprived of strong and independent political institutions at the Community level.

Federalists, on the other hand have believed that both these views were inadequate. They foresaw the limitations of an automatic and 'technocratic' path to political integration. They foresaw that this process would stop short when the forces supporting the existing nation states recovered their second wind. Only the additional force of a countervailing 'European' legitimacy expressed through an elected Parliament with real powers and supporting a strong executive could overcome the resistance to political integration.(3)

However, the logical problem is that this 'political power' must first be created in order for it to be able to perform the function which is expected of it. Up to now this has not been possible. Here the resistance to direct elections is significant. As we have seen, the opponents of direct elections have argued that direct elections will inevitably lead to the creation of a powerful European Parliament. They fear the creation of this political power. As will be argued later, it is by no means inevitable that direct elections will lead to the creation of a political power capable of transforming the structure of the Community. What, however, does remain certain is that no such political power now exists.

Thus, at this stage, the Community is reminiscent of a large construction project in an inefficient planned economy. The plan of what should be done exists, although some aspects of the plan no longer have the same relevance or importance as when drawn up; that plan is realised not necessarily in any logical order, but rather as the materials needed for any particular part come to hand. Other complementary or even necessary prior realisations are neglected if the means of realising them are not currently at hand. Progress is made where it can be made; some parts of the task are started and then abandoned. The élan and political impetus behind the project are being eked out in small doses and at times seem inadequate to the demands made of them.

This type of analysis can be particularly applied to the fragmented nature of the decision making process of the Community. It must now be evident that no single overall 'decision making process' valid for the whole Community exists, but rather a whole series of decision making processes, linked only loosely into a whole.(4) Some sectors progress but do so at their own autonomous rate without reference to the whole. For example, since 1973 the level of external coherence and the role of the Community in the world (the Lomé convention, the North-South dialogue, the Euro-Arab dialogue, discussions with COMECON) are the major bright spots.

142

The internal coherence and economic convergence are on
the other hand certainly less than in the late 1960s
(the collapse of EMU, the questioning of harmonisation,
the failures in the field of energy and transport
policy, new barriers to trade especially in
agriculture). Certainly it is a good thing that the
Community has progressed in respect of its external
policy; no one would wish to deny that. However, the
absence of any parallel internal development cannot
continue over an indefinite period. An overall
coherence must be exerted. If this will not occur
automatically by the progress of integration nor from
above, as the failure to respond constructively to the
Tindemans Report seems to show, can it come about
through the directly elected Parliament creating a new
politics at the Community level? This must now be the
key question.

The different analyses which have been made of the
reform of the Community institutions have assigned a
varying importance to the European Parliament within
their scheme. Some have regarded the Parliament as an
instrument by which the Community can be dynamised;
others have regarded other factors as the motive force
of the Community and have, therefore, only seen the
Parliament as an element of control or democratisation
of a process which has hitherto lacked a democratic
input.

This is not the place to analyse the proposals which
have been made from different sources and standpoints
for increasing the powers of the European Parliament.
We shall simply examine the two most extensive and
therefore most coherent sets of proposals: the
proposals contained in the Report of the Vedel
Committee (1972) and those made by Belgian Prime
Minister Tindemans in his Report on European Union
(1976).

The Vedel Committee was set up by the Commission in
late 1971 under the chairmanship of Professor Vedel
with two representatives from each of the six member
states and candidates (including Norway), reporting in

May 1972. It is worth recalling that the political atmosphere of the time was very different, though not necessarily in all ways more positive. There were then no prospects of holding direct elections, but the budgetary powers of the Parliament had recently been enlarged and the Commission was committed to new proposals both on budgetary powers (before the end of 1972) and legislative powers (before the end of 1974). At the same time, the enlargement of the Community to include the mature democracies of Britain and Denmark was expected to bring about a strong pressure for greater democratic control, far more powers for the European Parliament and a more 'political' Community.

The Vedel Committee based its report on two basic principles: democracy and efficiency. The Committee realised that any proposals must be realistic and would have to take into account the existing largely 'intergovernmental' development of the Community in the preceding period, which it was unable to see changing in the immediate future. A balance had to be maintained between the powers of the member states in the Council and the powers of the Parliament; between the powers of the Parliament and the independence of the Commission as an executive body. The Committee, therefore, proposed a system of co-decision which would be gradually extended over a widening range of the Community's policies, breaking down the distinction between 'obligatory' and 'non-obligatory' expenditure in the budgetary procedure since with co-decision the category of non-obligatory expenditure would no longer be needed to protect the legislative power of the Council and a role for the Parliament in the nomination of the Commission.(5)

It was proposed that in the first instance the European Parliament should have a right of co-decision in 'constitutive' acts (enlargement of the Community, agreements with third countries, Treaty amendments, legislation under article 235 of the Treaty of Rome). At a second stage the Parliament would acquire co-decision power over the harmonisation of legislation. On other matters Parliament would as now

144

merely be consulted. These new powers would have given Parliament considerably more importance. The atmosphere which had led to the setting up of the Committee was soon lost and no concrete follow up was given to the proposals.

The Report on European Union by Belgian Prime Minister Tindemans has of course to be seen as a whole - for that is what it is intended to be.(6) The atmosphere of 1974-75 was very different from 1971. Europe had lost its self-confidence; it was facing disintegration, the oil crisis and complete institutional stagnation. Mr Tindemans could not limit himself to merely 'institutional' remedies. For that reason the purely institutional proposals in the Report may appear more limited than might be expected. His proposals for the Parliament are limited, but interesting. He stated in his press conference, unveiling his Report that he relied on the dynamic of direct elections to strengthen the Parliament rather than detailed legalistic proposals. This dynamic operating within the framework, he proposed for European Union and taking on board a few new proposals, would enable Parliament to play a new and stronger role. Concretely, he proposed that:(7)

Parliament should be given (eventually by Treaty amendment) the right of legislative initiative,

Parliament should consider all matters inside and outside the Treaties, relating to the Union,

Parliament should organise annually a 'state of the Union' debate in the presence of the chairman of the European Council and a number of invited politicians who are not members of the European Parliament.

These proposals are modest but useful. They would not of themselves radically alter the status of the Parliament. However, the right of initiative would give the Parliament a more active and less passive and reactive role.

The reality has been different. Over the last few years debate has focused almost entirely on the Parliament's budgetary powers and the use which could be made of them, which is of course the classic route travelled, often over many centuries, by national parliaments. Parliament itself has frequently tried to graft elements of the Vedel conception into discussions about its budgetary powers or has adopted over elaborate institutional schemes which were expressions more of an institutional ideal than realistic proposals for immediate consideration.

It is most instructive here to examine the proposals on the Parliament's budgetary powers in order to grasp the interplay between a range of concepts in this field. Even after the 1965 crisis it was still possible to link the system of 'own resources' financing to an increase in the budgetary powers of the Parliament. However, the Parliament soon stood fast on the new principle that there was an inevitable link between budgetary powers and the adoption of legislation with financial implications. This was an alternative strategy. In the debate on Parliament's budgetary powers at the time of the 1965 crisis and preceding the signature of the Treaty of Luxemburg (1970) the Parliament concentrated on obtaining formal budgetary powers in the framework of the annual budgetary procedure. Here the member states could not concede much in the area of expenditure arising from Community legislative acts; otherwise Parliament would obtain a crude, but effective de facto veto over many decisions via the budget. It was from this impasse that the distinction between 'obligatory' expenditure (arising from legislation) and 'non-obligatory' expenditure arose and was enshrined in the Luxemburg Treaty. In the area of non-obligatory expenditure the Parliament has the last word within the limits of a fixed annual rate of expansion.(8)

At the time of the signature of the Treaty of Luxemburg, the Commission pledged itself to present new proposals within two years. This was finally done in June 1973. The Commission's proposals were not very ambitious.(9) The situation was certainly not favourable and the emphasis had shifted - under British pressure - to emphasise the need to provide for parliamentary control of the execution of the budget, hence the proposal for an Audit Court.

Parliament then seized on the need to enlarge the powers of Parliament over acts with financial consequences, given that the distinction between non-obligatory and obligatory expenditure could not be abandoned. Various formulae were suggested. Mr Spénale the rapporteur of the Budgets Committee, proposed that after a shuttle between Parliament and Council, Parliament should have the last word by a three-quarters majority (other majorities were also proposed). Mr Kirk suggested that neither body should have the last word and that joint agreement would be required. The view which finally prevailed was that of Mr Aigner, that the procedure laid down in article 149(1) of the EEC Treaty should be adopted. The Council would only be able to adopt an act against the wishes of Parliament if it did so unanimously after a conciliation procedure had failed. Even one abstention would have prevented the Council from passing over the Parliament's view.(10)

In the event, the most that could be obtained, was the Treaty establishing an Audit Court and providing for minor procedural increases in Parliament's budgetary powers and the Joint Declaration of the Three Institutions, establishing the concertation procedure. Under this procedure the Commission must specify in making a proposal, whether it meets the criteria laid down (an act with important financial consequences, of a general character). If the Council then intends to deviate from Parliament's opinion, the concertation procedure can be opened on the initiative of both Parliament and Council. In this procedure, all the nine ministers, the Commission and the Parliament's delegation (President, Budgets Committee chairman, Committee rapporteur and other appointed members) meet.

The Institutions attempt to reach agreement, but the

Council retains full power to adopt the act in whatever form it desires. This new procedure, while it does offer some real opportunities to the European Parliament, falls far short of the legislative powers that the Parliament has sought. It was, however, as much as could reasonably be obtained in the political climate of the period. It confirms, too, the more general tendency for a marked increase in relations and 'political dialogue' between the Parliament and Council.

Given the considerable expansion in the importance of the external relations of the Community, (the North-South dialogue, the Lomé Convention, the Euro-Arab dialogue, special relations with such widely differing countries as Canada, Israel, the Magreb and Mashrak States, Iran, Mexico, the United States and the People's Republic of China) it was quite natural that the Parliament should seek a greater role in this area and indeed a relatively more important role than national parliaments have in foreign policy making. Much has already been done following the Davignon and Copenhagen Reports to inform Parliament, or more precisely its political committee of developments in the field of political cooperation, on a regular quarterly basis.(11)

In addition, since the 1974 Summit Conference, the President in office has answered questions falling under the political cooperation machinery and normally there are one or two such questions each session. The proposal in the Tindemans Report to abolish completely the distinction between 'political cooperation' and 'Community matters' would increase the role of the Parliament in the external relations field. The so called 'Luns-Westerterp' procedure under which the Committees of Parliament are informed of agreements which the Community has initiated (but not signed) also gives the Parliament some oversight of external policy, at least as it appears in agreements. However, under these procedures the influence of Parliament cannot be very great. Furthermore, the financial obligations of such agreements, if in the future included in the budget, would in their very nature be 'obligatory expenditures' and hence escape from the control of Parliament.

In his draft report on the powers of Parliament Mr Kirk proposed that external agreements should be subject to formal ratification by Parliament. Such an enlargement in the present powers of Parliament would require the amendment of the Rome Treaty. It is for the moment unlikely that the Council would be able to accept such a change, however, it is an issue which will be on the agenda for discussion with a view to finding some means of increasing the powers of Parliament over external relations.

The Tindemans Report (as had the Vedel Report) proposes to give Parliament a role in the appointment of the Commission.(12) Mr Tindemans recognised, as had others before him, that the censure motion was a purely negative weapon and that the Parliament needed complementary 'positive' powers. He, therefore, proposed that the European Council would designate a president-elect of the Commission in the Autumn in advance of his term. He would obtain a vote of confidence from the Parliament and then form his team of commissioners, following certain basic rules as to national representation. As a first step Mr Jenkins was designated early and was able to consult with national governments on the persons to be appointed by them to the Commission. The role of Parliament in this has not been increased, but one element of Mr Tindemans' idea has already operated for the 1977-1981 Commission.

These then are the recent parameters of debate about the powers of the European Parliament. What use has it made of its powers, and what greater use could it make of them? This is an important point because, as we shall examine in more detail, it is likely that increases in Parliament's powers will not come from 'great leaps forward', but rather from a gradual organic growth as usage dictates. Overall, Parliament will have to build on its present powers, accidental and almost random historical accumulation though they may be, and will have to build up the case for more powers brick by brick on evidence both of a need for a given power and on evidence of responsible and full use of existing powers.

Our analysis will concentrate on three areas: control, legislation and budgetary powers. The main instruments of control are parliamentary questions, committee investigation and the motion of censure. The written question, now approaching 950 per year is the device of a small number of backbenchers, many of whom have specialised in this form of parliamentary activity, over a long period. One can mention Mr Vredeling (1958-73), Lord O'Hagan (1973-75), Mr Cousté, Mr Osborn, Mr Dondelinger, Mr Lagorce, Mr Pisoni, Mr Martens. Given the nature of the replies, members can obtain information and confirmation of positions from the Commission or Council, but rarely fresh action or statements of position. However, in the competition field in particular, a number of investigations were launched as a result of PQ's. Since it was introduced in January 1973, question time has become an important feature of parliamentary life. There are now over 250 questions per year. Since December 1976 there have been two question times (1½ hours each) per part sitting.

Committees frequently hold discussions with Commission officials and even commissioners on the execution of existing policy, often on the basis of regular reports which have been sent to Parliament such as the annual reports of the various Community funds or those made under certain other regulations. More recently, the establishment of the Control Subcommittee of the Budgets Committee has been a major innovation. Parliament shares with Council the power to give the Commission its discharge on the execution of the budget. Under the 1975 Treaty, Parliament alone will exercise this power. The Audit Court too, when established, will report to Parliament and undertake investigations requested by it. Up to now, the 'Control Subcommittee' has not functioned as a fully

independent public accounts type committee, but has
remained subordinate to the Budgets Committee. This
has not prevented it undertaking detailed
investigations of some areas of expenditure, especially
suspected frauds relating to the CAP. It has also
asserted strongly, even to the point of tabling a
censure motion, its right to obtain documents from the
Commission.(13)

The censure motion is in fact a very blunt
instrument. The Treaty imposes a two-thirds majority
of those voting and a majority of the members of the
Parliament (currently one hundred).(14) This means
that a motion must have the support of at least three
of the larger political groups if it is to pass. Even
though the legal arguments raised by the UDE group in
December 1972 to the effect that a censure motion can
only be tabled against the 'administrative failure' of
the Commission and not for a political reason, is no
longer held seriously, members are unwilling to
contemplate a censure motion without very serious
reasons for doing so. This view is reinforced by the
fact that, in the main, the Commission and Parliament
have been natural allies, mutually supporting each
other against the reluctance of member states to force
the pace of integration. Furthermore, and perhaps more
seriously, Parliament has no control over the
appointment of commissioners. They are named by the
member states in joint agreement. Would member states
agree with the judgement of Parliament and, following
the adoption of a censure motion, appoint a Commission
likely to be more acceptable to Parliament? One cannot
tell; at all events the political complications would
be considerable. Up to now three censure motions have
been tabled, but only one has been brought to the vote,
and in fact heavily defeated. Interestingly enough,
all have been tabled in the last six months of a
Commission's life which gave an added argument to those
who were opposed to the motion. Two motions (by Mr
Spénale in December 1972 and by Mr Aigner in December
1976) have concerned non-fulfillment by the Commission
of a (punctual) obligation to the Parliament: to make
proposals on Parliament's budgetary powers and to hand

over an internal financial control document on the malt sector. The third motion, tabled by the conservative group, was tabled as a critique of policy in the dairy sector. The conservative group, unlike the groups dominated by continental MPs, regarded the censure motion as a parliamentary weapon there to be used and were indifferent to these kind of considerations and even to whether or not there was broad based support for the motion. All three cases provided illustrations of the reluctance of MPs to adopt a censure motion and tactics by groups designed to replace the motion by a compromise resolution. One can say that a doctrine of the censure motion is only evolving gradually and with difficulty.(15) However, in the last few years there are signs that Parliament may be seeking a closer relationship with the Council and hence adopt an even handed position towards the other two.

In the legislative area Parliament issues opinions on draft legislations of the Commission. The problem of influence is a dual one: on the Commission and on Council. The Parliament must in the first instance examine the draft in committee, and if necessary work out amendments. This, as we have seen, is a complex process, in which the responsible Commission officials play a full part. The need for amendments or for new wider ranging proposals may be admitted informally by the Commission even at this stage. At the more formal level the Commission has established a follow up procedure on amendments posted in plenary. The Commissioner must state his view on the amendments and if he accepts them, the Commission must table amended proposals to Council. For 1975 and 1976 Parliament accepted opinions on 281 proposals, without amendment in 207 cases. In the other 74 cases, the Parliament's amendments were wholly or partially accepted in 52 cases. Only then in 22 cases were the amendments rejected by the Commission.(16) As a general rule it can be said that Parliament has had the greatest influence on matters such as company law reform (where the formula for worker participation proposed by Parliament was accepted by the Commission) and consumer protection.

Of course, even if the Commission modifies its proposal, there is no guarantee that the Council will approve Parliament's amendments. Even where the Commission does not amend its proposal, the Council and its subordinate organs have the opinion of the Parliament and may act upon it. Much will depend on the attitude of individual governments as to whether they wish to accept the opinion; some governments may find in the amendments adopted by Parliament backing for their own case. This has often been the case in respect of agricultural price proposals. As we have seen, where the conditions are met, Parliament may invoke the 'concertation procedure' which opens a more extended dialogue with the Council and indeed with individual ministers. Even so Council is not obliged to accept any compromise with Parliament. There have been too few cases, outside the budgetary procedure and direct elections to enable any meaningful evaluation of the concertation procedure to be made.

Frequently though the problem is much wider than these technical aspects. Parliament is passive. The Commission decides on the proposals it will make. Parliament has no direct right of initiative and even informally its 'agenda setting function' is limited. The Commission's 'programme' comes from a wide variety of sources: the European Council, member states, pressure groups, the Treaty itself and the pressure of outside events. Parliament has only a marginal influence on that programme. Parliament, because it is not a legislative body, rarely rejects outright any proposal, but frequently has expressed regret at the delay in presenting proposals or their narrowness and minimalist character. Parliament's criticism of the Council is often less that it has not followed Parliament's opinion, than that it has adopted nothing at all. In all this Parliament suffers palpable frustration.

The complexity of the budgetary procedure is such that each year new procedural and legal issues present themselves.(17) The procedure has been described in chapter 1. What we shall examine here is the reality of the budgetary powers of Parliament. Parliament has three basic powers in the budgetary process:

to amendment (within its margin of manoeuvre) non-obligatory expenditure (DNO);

to propose amendments to obligatory expenditure (DO);

to reject the budget en bloc.

The exact classification of expenditure as between DO and DNO is very complex and contested. One can say that the DNO lower the administrative expenses of the Communities, information policy, food aid programmes, the social fund, energy research. Parliament can reallocate and increase global expenditure over the DNO category, within the limits imposed by the Parliament's margin of manoeuvre which is calculated as follows:

1. each year the Commission must fix before 1 May the maximum rate of increase by reference to objective indicators of GDP and public expenditure in the member states. For 1976 this figure was 17.3 per cent. This figure is the maximum rate of increase for DNO as a whole. If the Council utilises more than one half this amount in fixing the level of DNO in adopting the budget Parliament may add up to half that amount. The absolute maximum rate of increase is, therefore, (in an extreme case) 150 per cent of the objective maximum rate fixed by the Commission.
2. The amount available to the Parliament must be calculated by reference to DNO in the last budget plus any supplementary budgets adopted during the financial year.

```
example:   DNO year 1              =  1000
           supplementary budgets  =   200

                          Total DNO year 1 = 1200

           maximum rate in year 2 = 15 per cent
           maximum increase       = 180
```

If Council adds X, being less than 90, then
Parliament may add (180 - X),
If Council adds Y, being more than 90, Parliament
may add 90.
Absolute maximum = 150 per cent of 180 = 270, the
maximum total DNO is therefore 1470.

It may be supposed that if the Council sent to
Parliament a budget in which total DNO was lower than
the previous year, then the margin for manoeuvre of
Parliament would be:

(DNO year 1 + 180) - (proposed DNO year 2)

which could be greater than 180.

By joint agreement, Council and Parliament can, under
article 203(8) go beyond the maximum rate fixed by the
Commission. Here it is to be supposed that Parliament
and Council would agree on a new level of DNO in our
example of say 290 which would then automatically be
translated into a new rate of 24.17 per cent.

Thus classification of expenditure is important for
two reasons: first, if it is a DNO, the Parliament has
the last word over that item and secondly its volume
adds to the level of DNO for that budget and hence
increases the margin of manoeuvre in future budgets.
Amendments have usually been tabled to considerably
exceed the margin of manoeuvre and the Budget Committee
has to make real political choices, subject to
ratification in plenary. The focal role of the Budget
Committee is becoming even more pronounced. Limited to
a margin which has since 1974 (when the new powers
became effective) varied between about 90 mua and 122
mua in 1976, Parliament has sought to achieve small
practical, but at the same time symbolic objectives
such as an increase in social fund appropriations, in
appropriations for nuclear fuel and hydro-carbon
research, and increased aid to the Third World.

There has been legal controversy about the ability of
Parliament to create new activities in the absence of
prior legislation, through new budgetary items. The
Commission must execute the budget, but can only do so

where a legislative basis exists. Where no such basis
was necessary or where the treaties provided one
directly, no problem would arise; otherwise (as in the
famous case of subsidies to the bee-keepers) nothing
could be done without a new basic regulation.(18)

On obligatory expenditure, Parliament can only force
the Council to deliberate again. As from the
ratification of the Budgetary Powers Treaty in 1975,
the Council will have to find a majority to reject the
proposed amendment. In this situation, the
concertation, with all ministers present between
readings could gain in importance. It should be noted
that in its budgetary deliberations, the Council does
in fact vote by qualified majority. The Parliament
certainly has very limited powers in respect of
obligatory expenditure, in particular in respect of the
cost of the common agricultural policy. Up to now,
Parliament has been relatively unsuccessful in pressing
its amendments on the Council. Over the years, no
amendments on the CAP have been accepted. For the 1977
budget, only three mua have been added to the total of
obligatory expenditure.(19)

Parliament has the power to reject the budget in
toto. This power is explicitly written in the 1975
Budgetary Powers Treaty.

The Parliament did not obtain, as it had demanded,
(20) the right to reject not only the whole budget en
bloc, but also individual chapters. Such a power
would have in effect given Parliament a power of veto
over expenditure on the common agricultural policy,
which it could use with impunity since it would not, as
now have to accept, at the same time, the political
responsibility of provoking a crisis. Rather in the
same way as the motion of censure, this power is rather
difficult to use. Were Parliament to reject the budget
in toto this would occur on second reading at its
December session. Since in theory the whole budgetary
procedure would have to be repeated, the next financial
year would open without a budget. Should this occur,
the institutions may spend one-twelfth of the previous

year's appropriation for each chapter per month - this
is the so called 'provisional twelfth system'. This
system would enable the Community to continue to
function until a budget was adopted which might take up
to three or four months. In a period of considerable
inflation and rapidly increasing agricultural
expenditure, there might be some embarrassment and a
decrease in expenditure in real terms. In this
situation the Council, Parliament and Commission would
have to find a compromise on which all could agree.
Here, at least, Parliament would have a power of
co-decision. Apart from the not inconsiderable
practical difficulties, rejection would signal the
opening of a serious political crisis.

This then is the situation. Parliament has power; it
has not all the powers that a national parliament would
classically expect to have, nor has it always fully
exploited the powers that it does have. It is feeling
its way towards a role in the institutional triangle.
The question now is what will be the dynamic effects of
direct elections on this situation. The main factors
conditioning the development will be political will -
both in Parliament and in the member states - and
legitimacy. In the ultimate, Parliament will only
gain in power and stature if the political will is
there. The legitimacy arising out of election by the
people will help to create, reinforce and maintain such
political will. It is not to be expected that there
will be a dramatic breakthrough which will lead to an
immediate major increase in the powers of Parliament.
Rather, Parliament will gradually affirm its position.
Its powers will gradually be extended as the need
appears. It may well be that the present pattern of
distribution of power among the institutions is largely
accidental and corresponds to no theoretically ideal
model of the separation of powers or of democratic
control. It has to be said that the provisions of the
Treaty concerning the powers and role of Parliament are
relatively poorly thought out. The exact role of
Parliament in relation to the other institutions was
not clear. The authors of the Treaty, in providing for
direct elections, evidently intended the role of

157

Parliament to expand, but did not make it clear how this was to be brought about.

The Community, in its structure, clearly does not resemble a nation state, nor even a federal or confederal state. There is no clear distinction between executive and legislative power, between 'active' and control functions. Parliament cannot expect to resemble a national parliament to which it is not comparable and whose functions - especially in sustaining an executive - it does not have. The development of national parliaments rests in most cases on at least 150 years of parliamentary tradition, in some cases on many centuries of tradition; in all cases modern parliaments are the inheritors of the 19th century liberal ethos, however much that concept may have been watered down or diluted over the years. Under that view, parliaments have very wide (formal) competences over the whole field of legislation and budgetary matters. The reality is that under the pressure of the need for planning and rapid executive action in more and more fields which are the hallmarks of modern technological societies and as a result of strong mass parties and their cohesion and discipline, parliaments no longer exercise, except in legal theory, many of those powers.(21) At the same time, parliaments are facing crises of identity and adaptation. The erosion of one role and the absence of new creative patterns of parliamentarianism have often created a malaise, and a preference for form rather than substance. This then would be almost the worst moment for the European Parliament to insist on imitating national parliaments. On the contrary, it should seek to develop a European parliamentary tradition and a model adopted to the specific needs of democracy at the European level.

The Parliament has certainly already made considerable progress in this direction. Since the foundation of the Common Assembly in 1953, a European parliamentary tradition has developed certainly a great deal more quickly than in our nine nation states. The best aspects of the various parliamentary traditions -

question time, the committee system, political groups, etc. - have been surprisingly harmoniously blended together. Within about twenty years Parliament has succeeded in gaining a respectable place in the institutional triangle, increasing, as we have seen, its budgetary powers, its influence with the Council and its resonance with public opinion.

Direct elections will give a new departure and a more pressing direction to these developments. For the directly elected Parliament, whether in 1978, 1979 or 1980, will be a completely different political animal from the present Parliament. It will certainly be able to build on what has already been achieved and go much further.

The elected Parliament will be different both organisationally and politically. The dual mandate, though permitted will no doubt be phased out after a transitional period. The result will be a full time parliament of 410 members. These members will be a new class of European politicians. They will have chosen to make a career in European politics, at least for a period. They will have been chosen as candidates for a European election and will have fought and won a European election. These members will have no doubt about their political legitimacy nor will they be tributaries of the national political situation to the present extent. They will not have to look over their shoulders at the national scene all the time. Such members can be expected to devote themselves entirely to European political activity. Apart from European parliamentary duties, their work will consist of liaison with their national parliament, their national and local party, being available to pressure groups and to their constituents, for which they will probably be equipped with a small personal staff. A new political cursus honorum will open up: a permanent or temporary 'European' political career and that at the same time as (in Britain) regional politics are coming into their own. In Britain one can imagine regional/European politicians who are not involved in Westminster politics. It is likely that apart from a small number of 'political stars' such as Willy Brandt or Edward Heath, there will be a large influx of new and younger men. Such European politicians will have a direct and close involvement and identification in making the European Parliament a success.

Such a parliament will without doubt seek a different style and form of organisation. Prediction is difficult, but it is to be supposed that the elected Parliament will establish a permanent seat: either in Brussels, where like most national parliaments it would be in the same place as other political institutions, giving Europe a 'political' as well as a 'bureaucratic' capital; or in Luxemburg where its secretariat now is. Probably too, the number of sitting days will increase from the present fifty or so to either a Spring and Autumn session of several months or to three sitting weeks per month for say eight or nine months of the year (excluding for example July, August, September and December). Committee work too would become simpler, absenteeism would decline and agendas would become less heavily loaded. Since the number of proposals and reports to be examined will not grow to the same extent, more time will be available for each than at present. The Parliament might well give considerably more time to public and well publicised 'pre-legislative' hearings, enabling Parliament to increase its 'agenda setting' role and to develop coherent policies over a wide range of policies based both on expertise and political choices. Parliament would in this way become less purely passive and reactive and more creative and combative.

At the same time, the Parliament will have the chance to benefit from the new European politics. The creation of European parties and platforms, the debate about Europe which elections will inspire, the greater level of media interest will all aid the Parliament in politicising Europe, in increasing its legitimacy and claims for more powers, which must rest on two pillars: democratic legitimacy as the expression of the will of the people and effective use of the powers that the Parliament already has. The MEP will have a legitimacy

and a mandate which cannot be contested; he will too
face demands and pressures which will be the normal
product of a political debate. These he will have to
translate into action. Pressures will, therefore,
exist in an elected Parliament which have hitherto been
relatively absent. Parliament will seek to affirm
itself as an institution. A sense of being an
institution - a sense of the 'House' - will develop.
Pressure for more powers will grow out of the need to
meet demands and expectations for which the present
powers are inadequate, even when used to the full.

In the British context, at least the development of
regional politics will make this easier. Scottish,
Welsh and Northern Irish MEPs, regardless of party and
no doubt some English members, will regard themselves
as regional representatives and regional assemblies
will no doubt seek to enter into some form of liaison
with them.(22) Without espousing extreme Europeanist -
devolutionist positions, it is evident that regional
politics are by their very nature indifferent to the
conservation instincts of Westminster and Whitehall.
For a regional politician - and institutionalised
regional politics in any case is a major constitutional
revolution, is naturally open minded in seeking to
solve his region's problems at the regional, national
or European level or all at once in differing degrees.

What might be the immediate priorities of such an
elected parliament in the course of the first and
second legislatures? These might be:

   a. to increase the prestige of Parliament among
   interest groups and opinion leaders active at the
   European level and in the member states by hearings
   and other research methods.
   b. To develop coherent policies, if necessary in
   opposition to the other institutions, over a small
   but key range of strategic areas: agriculture,
   employment, workers participation, multi-national
   companies, relations with the Third World. These
   policies would represent clear political options -
   those of a parliamentary majority after due

deliberation and examination of expert opinion.

c. In the field of external policy to press for closer participation in negotiation and conclusion of Association and other agreements with major political consequences. Such pressure could lead to forms of parliamentary ratification being accepted without Treaty amendment.

d. In the field of legislative activity, Parliament might by persistence and by the quality of its work, gain an initiative right such as suggested by the Tindemans Report. The concertation procedure should be used to pressure the Council into real negotiations with Parliament on legislation.

e. The range of non-obligatory expenditure should gradually be widened and the Parliament should attempt to negotiate with the Council regular increases in the 'maximum rate of increase'.

f. Parliament should seek participation in the appointment of the Commission. When intended appointments become known, Parliament can express itself formally by resolution. It could automatically table a censure motion when the new Commission presents its programme, in order to turn the following debate into a confidence debate.

Above all by its expertise, ingenuous use of existing powers and by its political legitimacy, it should not hesitate to create new precedents and obtain new concessions.

What can a directly elected parliament achieve? The answer will depend on the parties and the electors. The new European politics will effect the institutions and the member states, but as in all democratic decisions, the exact manner of that effect must be determined by the voters. Of course, an elected Parliament will be more powerful, of course the quantum of democracy will be increased. But it is not clear whether, at one level the new Parliament will constitute a political force in the Community acting as a counterweight to the member states, in some sense recovering an earlier vision of the Community, or

whether such a Parliament will be profoundly suspicious
of the old style integration. One can at least ask the
question whether with an elected Parliament with real
power, the Hallstein Commission would have achieved
some of its successes in the early 1960s. No one
knows.

At another level will the elected Parliament, as many
on the left hope, constitute a political riposte to the
technocratic capitalist and bureaucratic form of the
Community? Will direct elections open the way to a
more social Europe with new instruments of political
intervention to match?

Answers to both these questions must depend on the
sovereign will of the electorate. The people of
Europe will be given a voice in the construction of
Europe which has often been for them, but without them.
How they use that voice they must decide. Europe is at
a crossroads; it faces the acid test. The nature of
the Community, so long indeterminate - political or
bureaucratic, intergovernmental or transnational - is
about to be clarified; as is its growth, stagnation or
decline, by the first European election of 1978/79 or
1980 and in the European Parliament to emerge from that
process.

NOTES

(1)   Ernst Haas, an important theorist, admits this in
a paper presented to the APSA Annual Meeting (1975)
entitled: The obsolescence of Integration Theory.
(2)   Some theorists made a distinction between 'high
politics' and 'low politics'.
(3)   For example A. Spinelli: The Eurocrats: Crisis
and Compromise in the European Community, John Hopkins
Press, 1966.
(4)   This is well illustrated in Policy making in the
European Communities, eds. Wallace, Wallace and Webb,
John Wiley, 1976.
(5)   See Report of the Committee on the enlargement of
the powers of the European Parliament (May 1972),

especially p.100ff.

(6) <u>European Union</u>, published in Bulletin of the European Communities, supplement 1/76.

(7) <u>Bulletin</u>, supplement 1/76, pp.29-30.

(8) See Fitzmaurice op.cit. chapter 14.

(9) Document Com. (73) 1000 of 6 June 1973.

(10) See Debates of the EP, official Journal annexe 166, October 1973.

(11) Eds. Wallace, Wallace and Webb op.cit. ch.11.

(12) <u>Bulletin</u>, supplement, pp.31-2.

(13) Statement to the press by Mr Aigner, 6 December 1976.

(14) EEC Treaty, article 144.

(15) See EP Debates December 1972, July 1976, December 1976, official journal.

(16) Statement to Parliament by Mr Thomson, December 1976.

(17) See EEC Treaty article 203 and Reports by Lord Bruce of Donnington, general rapporteur for the 1977 Budgets, EP Document 472/76.

(18) Mr Cheysson, to Parliament, 14 December 1976.

(19) Lord Bruce to Parliament, 14 December 1976.

(20) See Mr Kirk, EP Debates, official journal annexe 166, p.14.

(21) Note by Professor Coombes in <u>European Integration and the Future of Parliaments in Europe</u>, Luxemburg 1975. English version pp.23-6, especially paras 8-10.

(22) This is recognised by the House of Commons Select Committee, Third Report.....para 42. Professor Coombes examines the more general issues in <u>Regionalism and Devolution in a European Perspective</u>, in Rowntree Devolution Conference Reports (May 1976) pp.15-22.

Appendix: The Act of 20 September 1976

DECISION
(76/787/ECSC, EEC, EURATOM)

The Council,

composed of the representatives of the Member States
and acting unanimously,

Having regard to Article 21 (3) of the Treaty
establishing the European Coal and Steel Community,

Having regard to Article 138(3) of the Treaty
establishing the European Economic Community,

Having regard to Article 108(3) of the Treaty
establishing the European Atomic Energy Community,

Having regard to the proposal from the Assembly,

Intending to give effect to the conclusions of the
European Council in Rome on 1 and 2 December 1976, that
the election of the Assembly should be held on a single
date within the period May/June 1978,

Has laid down the provisions annexed to this Decision
which it recommends to the Member States for adoption
in accordance with their respective constitutional
requirements.

This Decision and the provisions annexed hereto shall
be published in the Official Journal of the European
Communities.

The Member States shall notify the Secretary-General of
the Council of the European Communities without delay
of the completion of the procedures necessary in

accordance with their respective constitutional
requirements for the adoption of the provisions annexed
to this Decision.

This Decision shall enter into force on the day of its
publication in the Official Journal of the European
Communities.

ACT
CONCERNING THE ELECTION OF THE
REPRESENTATIVES OF THE ASSEMBLY
BY DIRECT UNIVERSAL SUFFRAGE

Article 1

The representatives in the Assembly of the peoples of
the States brought together in the Community shall be
elected by direct universal suffrage.

Article 2

The number of representatives elected in each Member
State shall be as follows:

Belgium	24
Denmark	16
Germany	81
France	81
Ireland	15
Italy	81
Luxembourg	6
Netherlands	25
United Kingdom	81

Article 3

1. Representatives shall be elected for a term of five
years.

2. This five year period shall begin at the opening of
the first session following each election.
It may be extended or curtailed pursuant to the second

subparagraph of Article 10(2).

3.   The term of office of each representative shall
begin and end at the same time as the period referred
to in paragraph 2.

Article 4

1.   Representatives shall vote on an individual and
personal basis. They shall not be bound by any
instructions and shall not receive a binding mandate.

2.   Representatives shall enjoy the privileges and
immunities applicable to members of the Assembly by
virtue of the Protocol on the privileges and immunities
of the European Communities annexed to the Treaty
establishing a single Council and a single Commission
of the European Communities.

Article 5

The office of representative in the Assembly shall be
compatible with membership of the Parliament of a
Member State.

Article 6

1.   The office of representative in the Assembly shall
be incompatible with that of:

   member of the Government of a Member State,

   member of the Commission of the European
   Communities,

   Judge, Advocate-General or Registrar of the Court
   of Justice of the European Communities,

   member of the Court of Auditors of the European
   Communities,

   member of the Consultative Committee of the
   European Coal and Steel Community or member of the

Economic and Social Committee of the European
Economic Community and of the European Atomic
Energy Community,

member of committees or other bodies set up
pursuant to the Treaties establishing the European
Coal and Steel Community, the European Economic
Community and the European Atomic Energy Community
for the purpose of managing the Communities' funds
or carrying out a permanent direct administrative
task,

member of the Board of Directors, Management
Committee or staff of the European Investment Bank,

active official or servant of the institutions of
the European Communities or of the specialized
bodies attached to them.

2.   In addition, each Member State may, in the
circumstances provided for in Article 7(2), lay down
rules at national level relating to incompatibility.

3.   Representatives in the Assembly to whom paragraphs
1 and 2 become applicable in the course of the five
year period referred to in Article 3 shall be replaced
in accordance with Article 12.

Article 7

1.   Pursuant to Article 21(3) of the Treaty
establishing the European Coal and Steel Community,
Article 138(3) of the Treaty establishing the European
Economic Community and 108(3) of the Treaty
establishing the European Atomic Energy Community, the
Assembly shall draw up a proposal for a uniform
electoral procedure.

2.   Pending the entry into force of a uniform electoral
procedure and subject to the other provisions of this
Act, the electoral procedure shall be governed in each
Member State by its national provisions.

Article 8

No one may vote more than once in any election of representatives to the Assembly.

Article 9

1.   Elections to the Assembly shall be held on the date fixed by each Member State; for all Member States this date shall fall within the same period starting on a Thursday morning and ending on the following Sunday.

2.   The counting of votes may not begin until after the close of polling in the Member State whose electors are the last to vote within the period referred to in paragraph 1.

3.   If a Member State adopts a double ballot system for elections to the Assembly, the first ballot must take place during the period referred to in paragraph 1.

Article 10

1.   The Council, acting unanimously after consulting the Assembly, shall determine the period referred to in Article 9(1) for the first elections.

2.   Subsequent elections shall take place in the corresponding period in the last year of the five year period referred to in Article 3.

Should it prove impossible to hold the elections in the Community during that period, the Council acting unanimously shall, after consulting the Assembly, determine another period which shall be not more than one month before or one month after the period fixed pursuant to the preceding subparagraph.

3.   Without prejudice to Article 22 of the Treaty establishing the European Coal and Steel Community, Article 139 of the Treaty establishing the European Economic Community and Article 109 of the Treaty establishing the European Atomic Energy Community, the

Assembly shall meet, without requiring to be convened, on the first Tuesday after expiry of an interval of one month from the end of the period referred to in Article 9(1).

4. The powers of the outgoing Assembly shall cease upon the opening of the first sitting of the new Assembly.

Article 11

Pending the entry into force of the uniform electoral procedure referred to in Article 7(1), the Assembly shall verify the credentials of representatives. For this purpose it shall take note of the results declared officially by the Member States and shall rule on any disputes which may arise out of the provisions of this Act other than those arising out of the national provisions to which the Act refers.

Article 12

1. Pending the entry into force of the uniform electoral procedure referred to in Article 7(1) and subject to the other provisions of this Act, each Member State shall lay down appropriate procedures for filling any seat which falls vacant during the five year term of office referred to in Article 3 for the remainder of that period.

2. Where a seat falls vacant pursuant to national provisions in force in a Member State, the latter shall inform the Assembly, which shall take note of that fact.

In all other cases, the Assembly shall establish that there is a vacancy and inform the Member State thereof.

Article 13

Should it appear necessary to adopt measures to implement this Act, the Council, acting unanimously on a proposal from the Assembly after consulting the

Commission, shall adopt such measures after endeavouring to reach agreement with the Assembly in a conciliation committee consisting of the Council and representatives of the Assembly.

Article 14

Article 21(1) and (2) of the Treaty establishing the European Coal and Steel Community, Article 138(1) and (2) of the Treaty establishing the European Economic Community and Article 108(1) and (2) of the Treaty establishing the European Atomic Energy Community shall lapse on the date of the sitting held in accordance with Article 10(3) by the first Assembly elected pursuant to this Act.

Article 15

This Act is drawn up in the Danish, Dutch, English, French, German, Irish and Italian languages, all the texts being equally authentic.

Annexes I to III shall form an integral part of this Act.

A declaration by the Government of the Federal Republic of Germany is attached hereto.

Article 16

The provisions of this Act shall enter into force on the first day of the month following that during which the last of the notifications referred to in the Decision is received.

Udfaerdiget i Bruxelles, den tyvende september nitten hundrede og seksoghalvfjerds.

Geschehen zu Brüssel am zwanzigsten September neunzehnhundertsechsundsiebzig.

Done at Brussels on the twentieth day of September in the year one thousand nine hundred and seventy six.

Fait à Bruxelles, le vingt septembre mil neuf cent
soixante-seize.

Arna dhéanamh sa Bhruiséil, an fichiú lá de mhí Mhéan
Fómhair, míle naoi gcéad seachtó a sé.

Fatto a Bruxelles, addì venti settembre
millenovecentosettantasei.

Gedaan te Brussel, de twintigste september
negentienhonderd-zesenzeventig.

ANNEX I
STATEMENT IN THE COUNCIL MINUTES

The Council is of the opinion that the provisions of
the Treaty establishing the European Coal and Steel
Community, the Treaty establishing the European
Economic Community and the Treaty establishing the
European Atomic Energy Community relating to the
jurisdiction of the Court of Justice of the European
Communities and to the exercise thereof apply to the
provisions of the Act adopted on 20 September 1976
under the same conditions as to the provisions of the
aforesaid Treaties.

ANNEX II
COUNCIL STATEMENT CONCERNING DENMARK

In view of the statements made by the Government of
Denmark at the meetings of the European Council on 1
and 2 December 1975 and 1 and 2 April 1976 regarding
the temporary derogations for the organisation of
direct elections to the Assembly in Denmark, that
Government may notify the Secretary-General of the
Council of the European Communities, when giving
notification of the completion of the procedures
necessary in accordance with its constitutional
requirements for the adoption of the Act, that:

   direct elections to the Assembly will take place in

172

Denmark at the same time as elections to the
Folketing. Until such time as the first direct
elections to the Assembly are held in Denmark, the
Folketing will appoint the Danish representatives
in the Assembly from among its members;

the Danish representatives in the Assembly must be
members of the Folketing, in particular so that the
term of office of a Danish representative in the
Assembly expires at the same time as his term of
office in the Folketing.

As soon as the situation permits, the Danish
Government will notify the Secretary-General of the
Council of the European Communities of the date on
which all or part of the above mentioned provisions
shall cease to apply.

ANNEX III
STATEMENT IN THE COUNCIL MINUTES

The Council takes note of the Danish Government's hope
of giving the notification mentioned in the last
paragraph of the Council Statement concerning Denmark
during the first five year period. The Council shares
this hope.

Index

References from Notes indicated by 'n' after page
   reference.
The term Parliament is used throughout this index to
   refer to the Assembly of the European Community.
The abbreviations MEP for Member of the European
   Parliament and EP for European Parliament are used.
Political parties commonly referred to by their
   initials are to be found under them.

composition of elected 13, 53, 160-1, 177; and decision making process 2-3, 8-26, 143-59; evolution of 6-7; on federalism 46; interest groups in 93-5; legitimacy of 7; and national sovereignty 28, 53; non-political members of 92-3; opinion of 11, 17-26; and member parliaments 27-42, 46-8, 57; present composition 1, 13-15; procedure of 16-26; powers of control of 9-13, 150

Parliamentary questions 10, 38

Parties, national political: accountability of MEPS to 127-30; development of European machinery 3, 97-119; and information channels 30; and rapporteurships 19; representation of 15-16, 61, 92; in direct elections 90-133; in elected parliament 123-5

Patijn, Schelto 57-8, 108, 128

Plaid Cymru 75, 86, 111

Pompidou, Georges 56, 58, 65

Portugal 5, 104, 111, 118

Prescott, John 86

Pressure groups 100, see also interest groups

Procedure 17-20, 23, 25

Procedure of Conciliation, see concertation procedure

Progressive European Party 106

Proportional representation: in Britain 76, 84; in Denmark 64; in France 66, 69;

Proposal, procedure on 17-20

Proxy voting 25

Question time 10, 24, 150

Questions, written 25, 150

Quorum 25

RPR 64, 69, 70, 118-19, 120

Rapporteurs 18-23

Referendum (British) 71

Regional list system 76, 85, 97

Regional representation: in Belgium 61; in Britain 71, 82, 86, 129-30; also 13-14, 60, 111, 161

Report 18-22

Representation: in elected parliament 53, 120-4, 162; and liberals 117; political 15-16; in present parliament 13; professional 14-15; regional 13-14, 60, 61, 71, 82, 86, 111, 129-30, 161

Resolutions 23

SNP 16, 75, 84, 86, 96,